WRITING FOR MANAGERS

EDWIN G. SAPP

University of Maryland-University College

Kendall Hunt
publishing company

Cover images © Shutterstock

www.kendallhunt.com
Send all inquiries to:
4050 Westmark Drive
Dubuque, IA 52004-1840

Copyright © 2011 by Kendall Hunt Publishing Company

ISBN 978-1-4652-0540-7

Printed in the United States of America
10 9 8 7 6 5 4 3 2 1

DEDICATION

What an apt word! My dear friends and colleagues, Dr. Cynthia Whitesel and Dr. Mark Parker are among the most dedicated professionals I know. Cindy was instrumental in building the University of Maryland University College's Writing for Managers course and raising it to become a national standard. She participated in the full-scale revamping of the course into an eight-week model and gave countless hours over a period of years to the creation of this textbook. Mark has moved heaven and earth to provide outstanding teachers in his role as Academic Director for Writing and Philosophy (and now, Interim Assistant Dean of the School of Undergraduate Studies), read and evaluated every word of the textbook you are now reading, guided it to a publisher, and ensured its publication.

And then there is Christine Adair, the Acquisition Editor for Kendall/Hunt Publishing in Maryland. Chrissy exhibited the patience of Job with the ups and downs that accompany such an undertaking. While Stefani DeMoss, the Senior Regional Project Coordinator, and Tammy Hunt, the Permissions Editor, both in Iowa, kept up with my flailing efforts to deliver chapter after chapter, the process evolved into a matter of months and more than 400 e-mails, numerous time-zone-synchronized conference calls, and a myriad of adjustments.

Saying thanks really is not quite enough. It surely is a true saying that "it takes an entire village…"!

CONTENTS

ABOUT THE AUTHOR

Ed Sapp received his undergraduate degree in English (with minors in math, music, philosophy, and psychology) from the University of North Carolina, and, two years later, his doctorate in law from that institution. Later he received his master's in English from Johns Hopkins and two master's-equivalent degrees from the Industrial College of the Armed Services (in National Security Management) and the United States Air Force (the Air War College).

Dr. Sapp has had practical experience writing to, for, and as a manager for over four decades. After time with his family's law firm and active duty service with the Judge Advocate General's office at Goodfellow Air Force Base in San Angelo, Texas, he began a career in intelligence. Along the way, he spent 27 years in the Air Force (11 on active duty) and 29 years at the National Security Agency (NSA) as a civilian. While at NSA, he was assigned to the Central Intelligence Agency (CIA)'s Office of Training for four years teaching Operations Research/Information Science techniques to intelligence analysts and received a fellowship to Congress for a year as legislative assistant to a member of the House of Representatives for six months and then to a Senator. He returned to NSA to be the director's liaison with four senate committees and wrapped up his service with that agency by overseeing a $1.4 billion joint service funding program for eight years, editing a 500-page budget request annually for congressional approval and preparing the Director's testimony for congressional hearings.

His intelligence experience included 11 years in Homeland Defense, including a recall to active duty to serve on the Air Staff at the Pentagon as the adviser to the Assistant Chief of Staff, Intelligence (earning promotion to colonel), and a final tour as the Air Force liaison to the Commanding General, First U.S. Army, Fort Meade, Maryland, for emergency preparedness and homeland defense in conjunction with 13 states, the District of Columbia, and three Federal Emergency Preparedness Agency regions. For this service, he received the Air Force Legion of Merit, a Meritorious Service Medal, and the Commander's Certificate for outstanding support from the Army.

After retiring from the Air Force and from NSA, Dr. Sapp continued an already extensive service as a professor for a number of institutions: the University of Alaska, Georgetown University Graduate School of Business, Johns Hopkins University, American University, Northern Virginia Community College, Anne Arundel Community College, Prince George's Community College, and—since 1993—the University of Maryland University College. Dr. Sapp also has taught for the CIA's Office of Training, the NSA's National Cryptologic School, Air Force Security Command, and in private industry (including an eastern seaboard plumbing supply business for which he trained employees from offices in five states to become better business writers).

Dr. Sapp's writing experience includes documents for the President, members of the Congress, the Secretary of Defense, a variety of senior executives and general/flag officers in all branches of the military, and the publication of more than 100 national-level, award-winning magazine and journal articles on subjects ranging from the acquisition process to antique automobile restoration, the authorship of three books, and service as senior editor for four others. He pitches his classes in business and technical writing (and this textbook) as exercises in writing as a survival skill. He and his wife Jeannie live in Calvert County, Maryland, and are the parents of eight children.

INTRODUCTION

Writing in a business environment truly is a survival skill. Unfortunately, it also is a skill many fail to develop because of fear of failure.

The self-doubt quite often begins in middle school when a student who is weak in grammar or spelling or agreement constantly receives poor or failing grades and learns to hate writing assignments. What most of us never realize is the majority of errors that people make in writing are clustered around a single principle. Thus, the person who consistently botches the verb "to be" will find him or herself with many red marks, aggregating to an abysmally low grade, for only one error! With the low grade eventually comes low self-esteem in regard to writing competency.

The "cure" for such misfortune always is worse than the error that caused the intervention. Invariably, a well-meaning teacher, unsure exactly where the errant pupil went astray, will begin again with "remedial" instruction containing all of the horrors that caused the student's problem in the first place. That simply is *not* the way to address such a simple problem and almost always drives the reluctant student to the hopeless conclusion that he or she will never "get it."

And so you may find that many of the people who work for you or with you have self-limited their opportunities in the workplace because of the lingering unpleasantness of significant failure in their youth. As managers, or as writers to or for managers, you should take the time to nourish the communication skills of others. Not only can you increase their self-confidence and productivity, but you also will strengthen communication in the workplace and between the workplace and the outside world.

Three major barriers impact managerial writing: failure to understand the problem, failure to communicate effectively with the reader, and failure to assess the impact of the communication *before* the arrow is sent on its path.

This is a course that focuses on these three barriers. Clear thinking is the foundation for effective analysis and the resulting clarity of expression. We will begin with this principle and carry the theme throughout the book. How often we see an eager employee snap off a rapid response in an e-mail, only to discover that he or she is "off-base" and has to rework the message completely to satisfy the request! Good analysis is the backbone of survival in the workplace and in the business world.

The writer who understands the problem but *assumes* that the reader is "on the same sheet of music" often leaves out key transitions and makes prodigious leaps of thought. Such writers often think that a *conclusion* is the same as proving a point. For example, writing "effective manager" on a résumé is merely an unsupported conclusion, and the writer would be in error to think the reader will be impressed, because the writer has omitted any example or result that would prove the empty claim.

Finally, this book focuses on the often dramatic and nearly often fatal (or at least tension-producing) results of a writer failing to realize that his or her communication to a manager, employees, or the public has been written in such a way as to cause a disruption in the Force. So, that is what this book is all about. It is *not* a basic business writing text, filled with forms, "thou shalts," and "thou shalt nots." It is not another visitation of those basic rules of grammar—and you will *never* find a single thesis statement in these pages, because managerial writing does not use that approach. The manager tells it like it is up front and then explains why. This book is a survival skills guide for a reader who can already write and now needs to fine-tune his or her approach to writing to, for, or as a manager.

Welcome, reader!

CHAPTER 1

Managerial Communication

A.   The role of managerial communication in organizations

B.   The fundamentals of effective communication

C.   Writing for decision making, action, and persuasion

D.   Ethical and integrity issues in managerial communication

> **True, This! –**
> **Beneath the rule of men entirely great,**
> **The pen is mightier than the sword. Behold**
> **The arch-enchanter's wand! – itself a nothing! –**
> **But taking sorcery from the master-hand**
> **To paralyse the Caesars, and to strike**
> **The loud earth breathless! – Take away the sword –**
> **States can be saved without it!**
>
> Edward Bulwer-Lytton, *Richelieu; Or the Conspiracy*, 1839

In some ways, managerial communication differs little from the everyday communication at all levels of an organization engaged in business. But in other ways there are significant differences in role (authority), tone, impact, and strategy. It is those differences that this book addresses. For the language of business communication's daily tasks, you must look elsewhere. This is *not* a business writing course.

Here we will focus on the core principles that distinguish managerial writing from routine business writing. Consequently, this book is intended to be short and *not* focused on the bells and whistles of tweeting, blogging, and other *current* manifestations of "modern" communication that have muddied the waters for the past decade—or the past century. When the dust settles, parallel line teletyping, e-mailing, texting, and tweeting, Skype, YouTube, and other social network media are identical in content and purpose, but far exceed the speed, bandwidth (or compression), and availability of the media they are replacing.

In the early 1950s, many organizations with work sites in remote locations used teletype circuits to transmit written material instantly. As a fail-safe precaution, and to permit two-way conversations, most organizations had two teletype lines to each outlying element. One line was reserved for "official" use; the other served as an emergency back-up and maintenance "chat" line. The operation was expensive (up to ten cents a character, in some cases), so operators developed the shorthand used in texting today (CUL ended a "call," for example). At first, management ignored the second line and then tried to restrict its use as "not work-related." Eventually, the second line function evolved into today's e-mail and intranet circuits (and, concurrently, came under even more control, regulation, and constrictive protocols levied by management).

Today, texting, tweeting, and social networks are evolving into managerial tools. Applicants now put résumés and achievements on Facebook and other web-based outlets for hiring consideration. The first step in a hiring screening now often is a Google, YouTube, or Facebook search to determine whether the applicant has written or said anything derogatory about a current or previous supervisor or displays questionable work habits ("so drunk last night I faked it at work all day today"). Skype has greatly expanded teleconferencing options from the more formal (and more costly) interactive teleconferencing circuits with their specialized equipment and location constraints.

The managerial writer who masters the concepts in this book will be able to select and adapt to any "new" vehicle without anxiety. The premise is that if you learn correct principles, you can govern yourselves.

A. The Role of Managerial Communication in Organizations

Writing to, for, or as a manager requires the writer to assume the role to understand what his or her reader is looking for. Managers routinely seek, interview, hire, and evaluate the workforce. They also discipline and fire employees, set policy, do strategic and tactical planning, respond to and anticipate crises, and make key decisions after reviewing issues and advice presented in point papers, white papers, fact sheets, memoranda for the record, and action memoranda. They review and set mission statements, vision statements, business plans, mergers, divestments, and a myriad of other things because of their authority and the necessity of the task. All of these things that people who write to, for, or as managers do have one thing in common: they change lives.

Audiences for managerial writing include writing addressed *to* managers from members of the work force, writing *for* or *as* a manager directed down the "chain of command" to workers; laterally to co-manager peers; upward to even more senior managers; or outward to another division, organization, or to the general public. Each one of these audiences has different expectations and requires a different organizational approach, tone, and signaling of the authority involved.

B. The Fundamentals of Effective Communication

The Communication Process

Aristotle described the communication process as a triangle involving the topic (*logos*), the writer or speaker (*ethos*), and the audience (*pathos*).

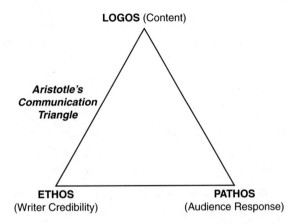

Even today, that three-dimensional concept works exceptionally well in helping a writer understand the forces at work when he or she attempts to compose a piece of managerial writing.

Logos

If the text is flawed because it is biased, incomplete, or in error, the results will not be as intended. American tobacco companies tried this approach on the public ("tobacco products do not cause cancer") for many years until the preponderance of the evidence to the contrary negated what turned out to be a claim and not a fact. The repercussions on the writers of such misstatements were severe, including penalties, loss of credibility, and distrust of the product, as well as the communication and communicators.

At the very beginning of the twentieth century, a determined group of scientists tried to block the building of automobiles with speeds up to 60 miles per hour because that speed would cause the human body to begin to disintegrate. In that case, unproven theory gave way to contrary proof when the Stanley Steamer and other experimental vehicles broke the "body" barrier and demonstrated that humans began to disintegrate only when the fast-moving vehicle impacted with a fixed object.

Ethos

The writer's credibility can be in doubt because of a past history (Aesop's "The Boy Who Cried Wolf") or position in the company (a worker advising a CEO). In such situations, to gain credibility, a writer will cite others with more credibility as having the same opinion. In this regard, the author may resort to surveys, citing recognized authorities, or even inserting the words of senior managers in his or her own organization as further proof that what the writer is offering is accurate and worthy of belief.

Pathos

The audience is the ultimate judge and jury concerning what the writer has written. The written word *must* be put in an expected format with a comfortable tone and foundation to be accepted. Acceptance also depends on the audience bias, attitude, past experience, and focus. Missing *any* of those marks can be just as deadly to a credible writer with a credible message.

Noise

Some communication texts also incorporate the concept of *noise* in this picture. Noise is the interference caused by other voices. However, from Aristotle's perspective, noise is never an issue in effective communication because a good writer *anticipates* the effect of external influences on a fragile audience and adjusts the presentation accordingly. A good example of this is the job applicant who tailors his or her résumé to meet the decision maker's needs and thus gains an interview over 500 other applicants (who constitute the "noise" that the writer is in competition with).

The Writing Process

Textbooks often describe the process as having only three steps: prewriting, writing, and revision. This is a dangerous oversimplification and invariably leads potentially good writers down the garden path. There are actually *seven* steps to the writing process, and ignoring any one of the steps can cause the writer tremendous difficulty in communicating with others. The steps are:

1. Obtaining the task.
2. Understanding the problem.
3. Organizing the communication.
4. Writing the draft.
5. Revising the draft.
6. Publishing the result.
7. Receiving feedback.

Obtaining the Task

In the world of business, *no one* writes without having a requirement (a task) to do so. That requirement might be self-initiated or it might come from others (your teacher requiring a paper, your boss requiring a report), but that step *always* initiates the writing process.

Understanding the Problem

It is not enough to understand the task, although, if understanding the task does not occur, then any response will be likely to be unsatisfactory. The soon-to-be writer must also understand what prompted the task. If your teacher tasks you with preparing a 500-word paper listing your professional development goals, before responding to what appears to be an easily understood task, you would do well to wonder *why* this particular type of writing assignment has been given. The answer to that *question* will almost guarantee you an "A," but the quick reaction to provide *something* most assuredly will result in a less-than-stellar performance.

The writer always has three choices once the rationale prompting the task is understood: (1) comply, (2) modify, (3) redirect. Anyone who has been in the work force for a decade or so has encountered a manager who wants a memo/letter/e-mail written *now* that would cause even worse problems than the one the manager is reacting to. In such cases, it would be wise to discuss strategy with the task requester *before* "adding fuel to the fire." There are other circumstances under which the action requested misses the mark and the writer can delicately turn the requirement slightly to make the action more doable or on target.

Organizing the Communication

Writers approach organization in a variety of ways. Some dash off a complete core dump onto paper or computer, then apply an outline to see what was left out; others spend time outlining in advance; and still others try for a mental outline and never look back. The word "outline" appears in every one of these approaches for a very good reason: a disorganized communication rarely gets the results intended and, even when it is successful, leaves casualties in the field.

The very word "outline" can cause an emotional reaction in some writers with exceptionally unpleasant memories of misspent youth trying to please the same teacher who insisted on perfect diagramming of some 10,000 sentences. But that is *not* the type of outlining necessary to assure the writer that he or she is in control of the product. A simple indentation is all that is necessary—no capital letters, lowercase, Roman numeral (upper- and lowercase), Arabic number convolution is needed here.

Writing the Draft

This is where "prewriting" ends and the buck stops shifting. The end of this part of the process is a newly minted, original *creation*. And stopping at this point of giving birth to turn in your creation nearly always results in a "C" in the academic world and in a so-so reaction from the boss at work. There is a lot to be considered in producing this key product of the writing process.

First, the writer who *edits* as he or she goes invites writer's block and invariably will delay the creation by a matter of *hours*. No other human will view your "raw" draft, so get the words on paper or on the screen *before* you "wordsmith" them and "lose the bubble" of concentration that will get you through the initial creative process. Do not correct grammar, rephrase sentences, or check spelling as you go. This one tip can cut your document preparation time in half and ensure that your first cut is closer to what is required.

Second, remember that writers are surrounded by beautiful models of the perfect paper. *Never* try to create such a paper from the first line to the last! That approach is analogous to trying to build a house by putting up the front door, then building the living room and so on *before* building the basement. Instead, develop the core statement or point of the paper *first*, and then add the other components. A good example is the difference between a good résumé and one that will almost never result in an interview. If the writer "builds" his or her résumé from a model, it becomes a generic biographical sketch. The company the writer applies for has listed a specific job and this version "looks OK" so it is sent, with no results. The writer who reviews the six requirements listed in the job ad, then builds a Qualification Summary (as a first step) that addresses each competency with a short statement containing an example and a result, and *then* "plugs in" the Locator information and adjusts the Experience entries so that each of the six competencies is highlighted *first* in each entry is much more likely to get the interview.

Remember that Newton's First Law of Motion works for managers as well as objects (an object at rest tends to remain at rest; an object in motion tends to remain in motion—*unless* external force is applied to it). Persuasion is that external motion, and it can have amazing results.

Revising the Draft

Now is the time to edit, revisit your outline, renew your understanding of the task, and reconsider the circumstances that led up to receiving the task. Revision is an iterative process—you cycle through all of the earlier steps until you have transformed the product from *writer-centered* to *reader-centered*. This process may take only a few minutes, but this is what produces excellent results instead of mediocre ones.

Publishing the Result

As part of the organizing step, you should have considered the audience needs and expectations. One expectation is the medium you have chosen to deliver your written effort. Electronic or paper? Abbreviated or lengthy? Sectioned or in one lump?

Receiving Feedback

"For every action there is an equal and opposite reaction" (Newton's Third Law of Motion). As some nursery tales would have it, "once you have awakened the beast," the beast will indeed respond—and respond with more tasking, most likely. Anticipating that equal and opposite reaction is quite important, because a good understanding will directly affect the nature and intensity of your future work.

C. Writing for Decision Making, Action, and Persuasion

Two axioms rule communication in the workplace today: (1) no one has time to write and (2) no one has time to read. Those two rules have altered managerial communication components. Today, managers value getting to the "bottom line" immediately, so decision making communication invariably begins with the action requested and then the reason why that action should be taken.

You may have heard that communication in the workplace is used to either inform or persuade. Before you try to distinguish the different types, however, you might contemplate the list of information types: the activity report, the trip report, a status report on a project, or a procedural or guidance memorandum might perhaps come to mind. Each one of these "informational" documents sets the reader up to respond in some specific frame of mind, and hence every one of these efforts may present information *primarily*, but they also do so *selectively* and thus have some degree of persuasion associated with them. What would happen to the middle-level manager who, in a series of weekly activity reports, listed only failures? How long would that manager be assured of keeping his or her job?

Managerial writing encompasses hiring, promoting, disciplining, firing, and training the workforce, setting policy, enlarging and downsizing operations (which include strategic and tactical planning, developing core value statements, mission and vision statements, business plans, and merger communication, acquisition memoranda of understanding, divestments), tasking, and responses to tasking. All of these activities require sensitive attention to audience reaction, legal and ethical implications, and strategy as initial components, with proper wording, grammar, punctuation, and basing writing skills a fundamental given.

D. Ethical and Integrity Issues in Managerial Communication

Truly, "the pen is mightier than the sword" (Edward Bulwer-Lytton) and it was Thomas Jefferson who encouraged Thomas Paine in a 1796 letter, to "Go on doing with your pen what in other times was done with the sword" (http://www.phrases.org.uk/meanings/the-pen-is-mightier-than-the-sword.html). Such power can result in terrible consequences if it is not wielded ethically and with integrity.

Core Values

The National Park Service Training Department offers this definition of Core Values:

> The core values of an organization are those values we hold which form the foundation on which we perform work and conduct ourselves. We have an entire universe of values, but some of them are so primary, so important to us that throughout the changes in society, government, politics, and technology they are *still* the core values we will abide by. In an ever-changing world, core values are constant. Core values are not descriptions of the work we do or the strategies we employ to accomplish our mission. The values underlie our work, how interact with each other, and which strategies we employ to fulfill our mission. The core values are the basic elements of how we go about our work. They are the practices we use (or should be using) every day in everything we do.

Core Values:

- Govern personal relationships
- Guide business processes
- Clarify who we are
- Articulate what we stand for
- Help explain why we do business the way we do
- Guide us on how to teach
- Inform us on how to reward
- Guide us in making decisions
- Underpin the whole organization
- Require no external justification
- Essential tenets

Core Values Are Not:

- Operating practices
- Business strategies
- Cultural norms
- Competencies
- Changed in response to market/administration changes
- Used individually (http://www.nps.gov/training/uc/whcv.htm)

The National Park Service states:

> **A strong and vital National Park Service grows from our mission and our values. Our mission gives us purpose. it is the expression of the ideals for which we all work.**
>
> **Our Core Values are a statement of the framework in which we accomplish our Mission. They express the manner in which, both individually and collectively, we pursue our mission. When we are challenged in fulfilling our mission, our Core Values sustain us and guide us in meeting the challenge.**
>
> —*National Leadership Council, 2001* (http://www.nps.gov/training/uc/tcv.htm)

The need for ethics permeates all aspects of business relationships and has two key guardians: the individual and the specific manager. Modern technology makes it easy for the least ingenious person to forge documents or manipulate information; the necessity of communication practices today give exceptional power and authority to the individual worker to act in the name of the organization, while managers "manage by exception" after the fact.

Consequently, a significant burden rests on the shoulders of the individual to be honest and straightforward in *every* dealing. The issues involved are so fundamental to the conduct of business that the majority of big businesses and the Federal Government have published Codes of Ethical Conduct for their employees. See http://usmilitary.about.com/od/justicelawlegislation/a/codeofconduct1.htm for an example of a description of the Code of Conduct for military forces if captured.

Home Depot Business Code of Conduct and Ethics

Home Depot has a business code of conduct and ethics that models these concepts thoroughly:

> Acting with integrity and doing the right thing are the driving forces behind The Home Depot's extraordinary success. From the very beginning, our Company has been committed to conducting its business in an ethical manner—doing right by our Associates, our customers, our vendors, our suppliers, our communities and our stockholders.
>
> The Home Depot requires its Directors, Officers and Associates to conduct themselves and the Company's business in the most ethical manner possible. We share the responsibility for protecting and advancing the Company's reputation, and ethics and values must drive our business strategies and activities. This Business Code of Conduct and Ethics provides you with the guidelines for meeting your ethical and legal obligations at The Home Depot.
>
> Doing the right thing while performing your job may not always seem the easiest choice or the most expedient way, but it is always the only choice and the only way. While our Business Code of Conduct and Ethics does not address every conceivable situation that you may encounter, it does provide straightforward information about the Company's operating principles and how Associates of The Home Depot are expected to conduct themselves.
>
> This Policy is not an employment contract or any other type of contract and does not modify the terms or conditions of any Associate's employment or benefits provided by The Home Depot.
>
> LIVING OUR VALUES. Our Values are our beliefs, principles and standards that do not change over time. Values are the resources we draw on when asked to make decisions. They form the groundwork for our ethical behavior. All that we do at The Home Depot must be consistent with the values of the Company. We believe in *Doing the Right Thing*, having *Respect for all People*, building *Strong Relationships*, *Taking Care of Our People*, *Giving Back*, providing *Excellent Customer Service*, *Encouraging Entrepreneurial Spirit* and providing strong *Shareholder Returns*. (http://ir.homedepot.com/phoenix.zhtml?c=63646&p=irol-govConduct)

Summary

Managerial communication differs from routine business communication in that its goal is to change lives. The functions that make managerial communication different from the routine business communication that govern the day-to-day details of running a business or an organization address the level and the function of the communication. Hiring, training, evaluating, disciplining, and firing the workforce, consolidation, disposing of property or elements, strategic planning, core values, mission and vision statements, business plans, and merger documentation are among the types of communication that are the subject of this course.

Effective managerial communication takes into consideration the relationship among the writer, audience, subject, and external forces present, plus adheres to the seven steps of the writing process. Although workplace writing has been categorized as informational *or* persuasive, in essence *all* workplace writing has some element of persuasion and, because of the authority and subject matter of such communication, requires the writer not only to have basic writing skills but expertise in understanding the problems addressed, the audience needs and expectation, and the ability to deliver the message required while minimizing the aftershocks.

Managerial writing often concerns itself with the development of core values and setting the policy they represent. Thee core values drive the creation of mission and vision statements—and help the organization to grow. The effective writer also adheres to ethical conduct principles and helps instill them in the organization.

POTENTIAL ASSIGNMENTS

1. If you are proposing a change in the way your organization does business, how can you strengthen your credibility (*ethos*), and what impact will your effort to do so have on the other two "corners" of Aristotle's communication triangle? Discuss in a paper.

2. Write a paper describing what happened when you tried to ignore one of the seven steps of the writing process and what you learned as a result.

3. Write a memorandum to your current supervisor. (Not employed? Write to a fictitious future supervisor in an organization where you want to become employed.) Describe your personal professional development goals. Use these three headings: Short-Term Goals, Mid-Term Goals, Long-Range Goals. Do *not* address your goals for organization development or production. Remember that these may be your *personal* desires, but you are also attempting to persuade the supervisor to acknowledge and approve them, so write for yourself *and* for the supervisor.

4. In a report to your teacher, describe the considerations you would have to weigh to deal with a low-performing employee. Your goal would be to salvage and return the employee to full performance; otherwise, to set the stage to dismiss the employee.

5. List five core values you would adopt if you started your own business and explain why each would be important to you, your employees, and your customers.

6. Why is a code of employee and ethical conduct critical in any organization today?

CHAPTER 2
The Language of Business Communication

A. Plain language

B. Reader-centered writing

C. Communication formats and strategies for managerial writing

D. Positive and negative messages

E. Persuasive messages

> **"A foolish consistency is the hobgoblin of little minds, adored by little statesmen and philosophers and divines."**
> Ralph Waldo Emerson (1803–1882), *Essays. First Series. Self-Reliance.*

Managerial writing has a different tone and content than routine business communication. The day-to-day responsibilities of running a business can generate e-mails, intranet messages, memos, and letters—all providing information, seeking to persuade or request or deny. However, managerial writing does these things at a level of final authority or decision making. When a senior manager "suggests" an action—that really is an order to deliver.

In this chapter, we will consider the need for plain language in managerial communication, a like need for reader-centered writing, the formats and strategies managers use to deliver positive and negative messages, and the concepts behind persuasive messages.

A. Plain Language

The National Partnership for Reinventing Government (NPR), originally the National Performance Review, was the Clinton administration's interagency task force to reform and streamline the way the federal government works. It was the eleventh federal reform effort in the twentieth century. In creating NPR on March 3, 1993, President Clinton said, "Our goal is to make the entire federal government less expensive and more efficient, and to change the culture of our national bureaucracy away from complacency and entitlement toward initiative and empowerment" (http://govinfo.library.unt.edu/npr/whoweare/historyofnpr.html).

One of the immediate outcomes of this initiative was a memorandum from President Clinton to the heads of executive departments and agencies.

The White House Washington

June 1, 1998

Memorandum for the Heads of Executive Departments and Agencies

Subject: Plain Language in Government Writing

The Vice President and I have made reinventing the Federal Government a top priority of my Administration. We are determined to make the Government more responsive, accessible, and understandable in its communications with the public.

The Federal Government's writing must be in plain language. By using plain language, we send a clear message about what the Government is doing, what it requires, and what services it offers. Plain language saves the Government and the private sector time, effort, and money.

Plain language requirements vary from one document to another, depending on the intended audience. Plain language documents have logical organization, easy-to-read design features, and use:

- common, everyday words, except for necessary technical terms:
- "you" and other pronouns:
- the active voice; and
- short sentences.

To ensure the use of plain language, I direct you to do the following:

- By October 1, 1998, use plain language in all new documents, other than regulations, that explain how to obtain a benefit or service or how to comply with a requirement you administer or enforce. For example, these documents may include letters, forms, notices, and instructions. By January 1, 2002, all such documents created prior to October 1, 1998 must also be in plain language.

continued

> • By January 1, 1999, use plain language in all proposed and final rulemakings published in the Federal Register, unless you proposed the rule before that date. You should consider rewriting existing regulations in plain language when you have the opportunity and resources to do so.
>
> The National Partnership for Reinventing Government will issue guidance to help you comply with these directives and to explain more fully the elements of plain language. You should also use customer feedback and common sense to guide your plain language efforts.
>
> I ask the independent agencies to comply with these directives.
>
> This memorandum does not confer any right or benefit enforceable by law against the United States or its representatives. The Director of the Office of Management and Budget will publish this memorandum in the *Federal Register*.
>
> *Source:* http://www.plainlanguage.gov/whatisPL/govmandates/memo.cfm

The movement caught momentum and eventually became the Plain Writing Act of 2010 (H.R. 946), which was signed by President Obama on October 13, 2010 (http://centerforplainlanguage.org/plain-writing-laws/plain-writing-act-of-2010/).

With all the emphasis in the government on plain language beginning in the early 1990s, perhaps an example will underscore why the effort came about and what it was attacking.

The year was 1995, and the Social Security Administration was trying hard to use the new guidance:

> ## Notice of Overpayment Form SSA-L8172
>
> February 27, 1995
>
> Mr. Xxx Xxxxx
> xxxx Xxxxxxx Xx
> Charles Village
> Baltimore, MD
>
> Dear Mr. Xxxxx:
>
> We are writing to let you know that we have paid you $6.80 too much SSI money.... You must pay us back unless we decide you shouldn't have to pay us back or we're wrong about the overpayment. If you think you shouldn't have to pay us back or you disagree with the decision about the overpayment, you can ask for a waiver, ask for an appeal, or do both.
>
> *continued*

You may not have to pay us back. Sometimes we can waive an overpayment, which means you won't have to pay us back. We can do this if both of the following are true: It wasn't your fault that you got too much SSI money and paying us back would mean you can't pay your bills for food, clothing, housing or medical care, or it would be unfair for some other reason. If you think these are true, contact any Social Security office. You can ask for a waiver any time by asking your Social Security office to fill out waiver form SSA-632. We won't collect the overpayment while we decide if we can waive it.

If you disagree with the decision, you have the right to appeal. We will review your case and consider any new facts you have. You have 60 days to ask for an appeal. The 60 days start the day after you get this letter. We assume you got this letter five days after the date on it unless you show us that you did not get it within the five-day period. To appeal, you must fill out a form called "Request for Reconsideration." The form number is SSA-561.

There are three ways to appeal. You can pick the one you want…. You have a right to review the facts in your file. You can give us more facts to add to your file. Then we'll decide your case again. You won't meet with the person who decides your case….

//four more pages//

There are many reasons writing is not plain. Among them are confusion in the mind of the writer, inexactness in word choice, and a failure to organize thoughts. Any *draft* produced as step 4 of the Writing Process will naturally *not* be plain writing if the first three steps (getting the task, understanding the task and the problem that generated the task, and organizing the response) are not precise.

Here is another actual example, written in 2004, well after President Clinton's initial push to make communication in the federal government more simple (the military organization letterhead has been omitted and the project name changed to protect the guilty):

Memorandum For: JADE PMO Personnel

Subject: Implementation of JADE Program CM Disciplines

1. The purpose of this memorandum is to emphasize the implementation of formal Configuration Management (CM) disciplines for the JADE Program.

2. The complexities, criticalities, and rapid development of this program make it essential that this formal CM discipline be understood and proactively implemented by all program elements. As Program Manager, I am requesting

continued

that all Government and contractor support personnel become fully knowledgeable in this discipline and conform to its direction and procedures, to include all related program activities. The CM discipline has my full support and I trust you will put forward your best effort to actively implement it in support of the JADE Program.

3. Constructing and implementing an effective CM Organization is a team effort which will benefit all of us, as well as being flexible to provide the best product/support to JADE users.

4. We have a qualified staff of IMS/CM representatives to assist, guide, and instruct on how to transition and conform smoothly to rigid CM disciplines. The following individuals are available to handle your CM issues/concerns: xxxxx, xxxxx, xxxxx, and xxxxx.

5. Additional IMS/QM representatives will be made available as required. Thanks in advance for your cooperation.

/s/
Colonel, USAF
Program Manager

The obvious first problem with the memo is that there is no date. All memos *must* have these four components to be useful: a date, the recipient's name, the sender's name, and a subject. Conventions in any given organization will have these components appear in a number of forms, but without those four ingredients, it is impossible to communicate effectively. Note that the lack of a date makes an implementation announcement completely worthless.

The format is okay. It was written by an organization that numbers paragraphs as a convention.

However, the writer of this memo has caused many more problems for his (this program manager was a male) readers. Above all, configuration management is *not* a discipline with disciples—it is a series of agreed-upon *standards* that assure the compatibility of components of a larger system. For example, it is an industry-wide agreement that assures that the new speakers you buy for your amplifier plug in the same way as the old ones and will not "blow out" when you turn the set on. All components made by all media equipment manufacturers adhere to the same configuration management standards.

But, wait! As the television hucksters say, there's more! In this memo, the subject line states that the memo is about the *implementation* of CM standards (mislabeled "disciplines"). The first line of the first paragraph, however, assures the reader that the topic is to *emphasize* the implementation. In reality, development of the JADE system began 12 years before, so this would not be a logical time for implementing standards that should have been agreed upon at the outset.

Finally, after ignoring the facts that "criticality" is not a real word, the phrase "the purpose of this memorandum is to" has no value or reason to exist, and that the phrase "as program manager" should not have initial capital letters, the writer cautions the readers to implement, actively implement, and proactively implement the CM discipline(s). (He can't seem to decide if "discipline" should be singular or plural.) Implementing is a one-time activity. It is not possible to inactively implement, nor is proactive activity any different than active activity or just plain old activity alone. The reader has been drowned in a sea of useless, large, and misapplied words.

Another area where plain language has made an impact in government correspondence is President Obama's hiring reform initiative of May 11, 2010. Effective in all agencies by November 1, 2010, this initiative eliminated written essays (Knowledge, Skills, and Abilities, or KSAs) in initial applications and replaced them with résumés and cover letters or just simple, plain-language application letters. "Americans must be able to apply for Federal jobs through a commonsense hiring process and agencies must be able to select high-quality candidates efficiently and quickly" announced the Presidential Memorandum.

B. Reader-Centered Writing

> **Blot out, correct, insert, refine**
> **Enlarge, diminish, interline.**
> **Be mindful, when invention fails.**
> **To scratch your head and bite your nails.**
> —Jonathan Swift (1667–1745), *On Poetry*

The fourth step of the seven-step writing process discussed in Chapter 1 introduces *revision* to what, up to that point, had been a predominantly *writer-centered* effort. Writer-centered drafts are the natural outcome of the creative process required to wrestle concepts to paper or the computer screen. As noted in Chapter 1, introducing any form of editing or revision before the final draft has been crafted is not only a waste of time but quite likely to result in a painfully slow and flawed creation accompanied by large segments of writer's block. Preemptive editing paralyzes the brain.

However, before the newly created creation goes public, it must be reviewed critically to see whether it addresses the *reader's* needs. If this step is bypassed, then the result will not be an effective piece of writing and may bring serious consequences upon the writer.

During the revision phase of the writing process, the draft should be edited for completeness, cohesiveness, grammar, spelling, and tone. Does it contain what the reader needs to see—in the order the reader will expect or must encounter to understand what is being communicated? Does the message raise any unnecessary red flags?

Here is an example of a simple note-style proposal to a manager. The writer has discovered a problem with the completion time for accountant-generated reports essential to the production elements of the company. He did some research and found that a specific accounting software package could cut the report-generating time cycle by 50 percent. So he sent his boss a short note (remember, "time is money!"):

Mr. Jones,

We need to purchase the MOTORGRINDER accounting software for our office. At only $1,100 per copy, our five accountants will benefit from a much more efficient process in having our Accounts Bookkeeping operate smoothly.

Joe

Joe was surprised when Mr. Jones said no and asked him to research other options. Other than the grammar problem (the accountants are not $1,100 a copy), what happened here?

Basically, Joe had produced a *writer*-centered note that succinctly stated his conclusions without taking Mr. Jones through the process. This might have worked better:

Mr. Jones,

Delays in receiving Accounting Department reports are impacting Production timeliness significantly. I recommend purchasing a more efficient accounting software package that should reduce report generation time by 50 percent.

Of five products I reviewed with the Accounting staff, MOTORGRINDER accounting software offers the most for the cost. At $1,100 per copy, it is more expensive than other options; however, our five accountants will benefit from a much more efficient process in having our Accounts Bookkeeping operate smoothly, and Production delays should disappear completely.

Joe

The second note should garner either an approval or a request to discuss Joe's cost analysis of the other four products. Either way, there were two issues to begin with: (1) whether the company should buy software and (2) if so, which package to purchase. The second note will gain agreement that software *should* be purchased and go a long way toward the boss agreeing to invest the $5,500. The first note lumped the two issues with the *assumption* that the boss would agree that software was needed. But the significant cost would make the boss throw out the first step (software is needed) with the second (a specific brand is the *only* solution).

C. Communication Formats and Strategies for Managerial Writing

Copyright (c) 1996 by Thaves. Distributed from www.thecomics.com.

The electronic age has ushered in many media/vehicle options to carry managerial communication but a surprisingly small number of format options, at least, in the generic sense. The common vehicles of such communication are the letter (to readers outside the organization), the memorandum (to people within the organization or in an interdepartmental setting), the note, and the report.

Of course, any one of these vehicles can be transmitted as paper, by hand, or electronically. All have in common the need for the four common ingredients of TO, FOR, SUBJECT, and DATE information; however, the convention of the organization dictates how this information should be displayed.

As noted earlier, all managerial communication must acknowledge two rules of engagement in almost every twenty-first-century organization: (1) no one has time to write and (2) no one has time to read. As a consequence, organizations develop "pro forma" standards such as a preformatted intra-office e-mail that compels the writer to provide FROM and DATE input automatically and won't send the message without a TO a or SUBJECT area completed. The creation of memos and letters often is controlled to the same degree.

The Reports category contains a large number of subspecies ranging from trip reports, status reports, personnel evaluations, disciplinary actions, memos for the record, white papers, fact sheets, action requests, short reports, and long reports—all requiring some degree of research and the inclusion of supplemental documentation.

In this chapter, you have seen several samples of memos in various formats as dictated by the organization that generated them. Following is a letter exchange between the Deputy Secretary of Defense and the Secretary of the Air Force. Note the letterhead format of this correspondence. This exchange was written in 1994 and printed on stationery that already had the seal and heading matter printed on it. Today, such correspondence is generated on forms stored in the office computer and no letterhead stationery source is required.

THE DEPUTY SECRETARY OF DEFENSE
WASHINGTON, DC 20301-1000

15 MARCH 1994

MEMORANDUM FOR: THE SECRETARY OF THE AIR FORCE
                 ASSISTANT SECRETARY OF DEFENSE
                 (PERSONNEL AND READINESS)

Subject: Sexual Harassment Policy Plan

Combating sexual harassment is an important element of our overall Department of Defense policy of fair and respectful treatment of our Military service members and civilians. The Secretary and I are concerned that the Department has yet to develop and implement fully the policies and procedures we need to rid the Department of sexual harassment.

Therefore, I would appreciate it if you would formulate a plan of action and a calendar for developing and implementing these policies and regulations. Your plan should take cognizance of those unique characteristics of each of the Military Services that bear on this matter, as well as a procedure for reporting progress to the Congress. I look forward to reviewing your proposal within 21 days.

Source: The United States Deputy Secretary of Defense and the Secretary of the Air Force, Sexual Harassment Policy.

SECRETARY OF THE AIR FORCE
WASHINGTON

25 APRIL 1994

MEMORANDUM FOR THE DEPUTY SECRETARY OF DEFENSE

Subject: Sexual Harassment Policy Plan

In your memo of March 15, 1994, you asked us to develop a sexual harassment policy action plan. The plan we have developed incorporates several initiatives and is rooted in our firm commitment to eradicating both discrimination and sexual harassment in the Department of Defense.

Secretary Perry stated in his Equal Opportunity memorandum of March 3 that "all employees of this Department have a right to carry out their jobs without discrimination or harassment. Our broad goal, when dealing with issues of discrimination and harassment, is to ensure that we create and maintain a work environment where all of our employees can excel. In the military services, we must make the Chain of Command work for service members and against discrimination in the military.

Our plan has five main elements. We will:

- Work with Congress toward our mutual goal of eliminating discrimination from the Department of Defense. Specifically, we will soon send the HASC our after action reports on the sexual harassment cases highlighted in the March 9 hearing. On April 20, Under Secretary Dorn sent a letter to Chairman Dellums reviewing lessons learned in anticipation of the individual Services' reports. We will also continue to cooperate with the HASC Task Force on Equality of Treatment and Opportunity in the Armed Forces.

- Formulate a new sexual harassment policy statement. This policy statement is now under review and will be ready for SecDef signature on May 15.

- Establish the DEOC Task Force on Discrimination and Sexual Harassment to review the military services' discrimination complaints system and recommend improvements, including the adoption of Department-wide standards.

- Initiate a new sexual harassment survey to ascertain whether service members have confidence in the current system.

- Implement senior leadership training at the Defense Equal Opportunity Management Institute. This training will include workshops on ending discrimination and sexual harassment.

continued

Discrimination and Sexual Harassment Task Force Mission Statement

Secretary of the Air Force Widnall and Under Secretary of Defense Dorn have established the Defense Equal Opportunity Council (DEOC) Discrimination and Sexual Harassment Task Force as a part of a five point plan proposed to the Deputy Secretary of Defense in response to his March 15 memorandum.

The mission of the DEOC Task Force is to examine and investigate the military Services and their Reserve Components' discrimination complaints processes through briefings provided, in part, by the Services. The Task Force will then review information gathered from the briefings and recommend improvements, including the adoption of Department-wide standards. A final summary report of its findings and recommendations will be released to the Defense Equal Opportunity Council (DEOC) in August for review and transmittal to the Deputy Secretary of Defense.

Source: The United States Deputy Secretary of Defense and the Secretary of the Air Force, Sexual Harassment Policy.

Note that the Deputy Secretary of Defense has issued a tasking letter that *must* be responded to. Senior management correspondence does not have to make demands or order compliance. The imperative nature of the task is transmitted by the knowledge of who the requirement is coming from. "I would appreciate it" is enough to get an entire staff working on a detailed response.

In this case, and prompted by recent public outcry regarding sexual harassment in the Armed Forces (look up "Tailhook" online), the Defense Department is asking for policy on a difficult area that has not been addressed before. The definition of sexual harassment came out of this era, as did a number of laws and regulations.

Note that the Deputy Secretary of Defense asks for four things:

1. A plan of action
2. A calendar for developing and implementing policies and regulations
3. The plan addressing the unique characteristics of each military service
4. A procedure for reporting to Congress

The suspense was 21 (calendar—not working) days from 15 March 1994.

Now read the Secretary of the Air Force's response carefully. You will note that the response:

1. Was signed on 25 April, 41 days after the task was written and 20 calendar days after it was to be provided.
2. Combines the sexual harassment task with Secretary Perry's 3 March task to address discrimination.

3.   Describes a plan with five main elements that includes "WORKING WITH the Congress, creating a Discrimination and Sexual Harassment Task Force, surveying service members, train leaders, and create a policy statement for Secretary of Defense signature (by 15 May—the only specific date on a calendar of implementation).

The delay in responding was occasioned by the significantly complex issues involved in dealing with regulations and policies addressing human conduct, plus the intervention of a national holiday (Easter). The survey is rather simplistic because members would not be likely to report that discrimination or harassment by their superiors still existed for fear of recrimination (remember, no guidelines then existed to punish managers who discriminated or harassed).

Most important in the response, however, are three items that *completely changed the tasking*. First, the second paragraph combines the two tasks that otherwise would have the Air Force forming two task forces and facing the risk of developing inconsistent policies on two areas that were related (sexual harassment, after all, is one manifestation of discrimination). When the Department of Defense accepted the response and its counterproposal without further response or objection, that changed the task.

The second change came with the Air Force simply ignoring the charge to create policy for the Army, Navy, Marine Corps, and Coast Guard. That was not in the Air Force charter and Defense should never have ordered them to do so.

The third change was in noting that the Air Force was *working* with the Congress, *not reporting* to the Congress. The Constitution of the United States set up *three* branches of Government: the executive, legislative, and judicial branches, to avoid conditions that could lead to a monarchy. Consequently, the legislative branch (the Congress) cannot *order* the executive branch (containing the Department of Defense) to do anything (or vice versa). The writer of the Air Force response might have reminded the Deputy Secretary of Defense, indelicately, that he had overstepped the bounds of the Constitution, but this response takes care of the entire issue by again *changing the tasking*.

Now you can see that the *forms* of managerial communication are quite simple, but the *strategies* are not.

Point papers or white papers generally present an *issue*, a recommended action, and the background that the decision maker should consider in deciding to adopt the recommended course of action or reject it. Formats vary according to industry or organizational needs and dictates, but the content usually includes the sections discussed previously in one or two pages. Detailed support may accompany the paper infrequently, but generally as a separate document.

Trip reports may be required when an employee travels for the organization. Generally speaking, this type of report contains the purpose for the trip, key people met, key issues, and any agreements or remaining issues discussed or developed. Because these reports are often in immediate demand upon the traveler's return, it is wise to write the entire report *in advance* and then modify it according to actual events on the return leg of the journey.

Memoranda of Understanding (MOUs) are like the action/conclusion end of trip reports, they list areas of agreement between two parties and are jointly signed. Trip reports and weekly (or some other period) activity reports purport to be *informational*, but in actuality, the writer always "manages" the factual content so as to set the stage for some sort of favorable reaction; hence these reports are actually *persuasive* in nature.

Short, long, and status reports normally address issues and what needs to be done about them or is being done about them. Long reports, in particular, most often are actually "packages" with components that are developed independently. These components consist of "front matter," the report, and "back matter." The component parts of a long report most often are (in this order):

1. The front matter, beginning with a letter of transmittal or a routing slip listing the author, the subject, the decision maker, and what the "package" contains.

2. A title page with the author, decision maker, title, and date.

3. An abstract (American Psychological Association, APA) or executive summary (Modern Language Association, MLA).

4. A table of contents listing the main sections of the actual report, the front matter, the back matter, and the starting page number.

5. A list of illustrations with the title of the illustration or graphic and its page number in the body of the report.

6. The report (which usually includes a number of "imbedded" illustrations or graphics appearing on the same page as the discussion) with component parts, usually including an introduction, discussion of the problem, background, suggested solution, additional recommendations, and a set of step-by-step recommended implementation steps.

7. The back matter (a Works Cited sheet [MLA] or References page [APA] and possible glossary and/or appendices).

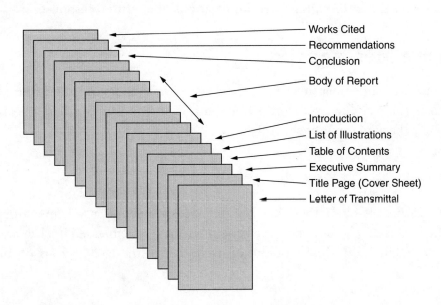

D. Positive and Negative Messages

Neither positive nor negative messages delivered for, to, or as managers are completely simple. The message may be *very* straightforward, but the effects of the message are quite often not simple at all.

At one government agency a few years ago, the House Appropriations Committee mandated a 10 percent cut in already staffed positions in a specific program and gave a deadline for the cut to be given. The director of the agency tasked his budget office to take the cut and the budget director sent a message to every element at the agency with positions affected by the cut asking them to rejustify the positions they held. The divisions were given ten days to submit their justifications (by noon on the Thursday before the Friday that a committee would meet to determine which positions would be cut). A recommendation would then be drafted that afternoon and delivered to the director the following Monday morning to be signed and delivered to the Congress before their noon deadline that day. The cut was nonnegotiable.

One element with two positions was the agency Inspector General's office. The Inspector General (IG) waited until 5:00 p.m. on the Friday *after* the committee had completed its meeting to send his response via courier, who announced that the IG was traveling and could not be reached for further discussion. The reply was two words: "Nonsense. Non-concur."

The IG was relying on his office's position in the agency structure (higher than the budget office) to intimidate the committee. The primary message was power; the secondary one was insult.

The committee recommended cutting the IG positions, and the director concurred. When the IG complained to the director Monday morning, the director told him that he should have complied with the budget office request, which reflected the will of the Congress. A writer *must* think through *all* the ramifications of a written response.

E. Persuasive Messages

A key factor to remember in writing persuasive correspondence is that your persuasion must be *reader*-centered. The argument is not about what you want; rather, it is about what issue or urgency the reader might see or feel.

Summary

In the past decade or so, there has been a extensive federal government–directed effort to have the language of policy and government business be expressed in clear and simple terms. The concept, although simple in and of itself, flies in the face of years of more convoluted communication patterns, so progress has been slow. Managerial communication must be more plain if it is to be effective, whether written for government offices, the general public, or commercial enterprises of any size or discipline area.

Writing produced by, for, and as managers must also be *reader*-centered to be effective in an era when there is too much communication to be absorbed and not enough time to write. Managerial writing appears in a relatively small number of generic formats with details dictated by disciplines and organizational customs; however, the strategies associated with such writing are designed to change lives. The writer must be sensitive to the side effects of such powerful writing or the results will miss the mark. In that regard, positive and negative messages—although simple in their content—are far from simple in their effects on the reader, so care must be taken in their creation and distribution.

Persuasive messages must be *writer*-centered to be effective. The writer must remember that it is the *reader's* problem that must be addressed—not the writer's, if action is to be had.

POTENTIAL ASSIGNMENTS

1. Discuss an unclear policy or guidance letter, memorandum, or e-mail that you have received and what happened as a result of the confusion it caused. Attach a copy of the message, if it is available.

2. Change this internal memorandum from an agency director to be *reader*-centered:

> The Agency will be conducting its annual Combined Federal Campaign (CFC) from October 7 through November 15. The campaign theme is "The American Spirit is the key to the CFC."
>
> The Agency has been the major contributor to the CFC in this state for the past several ears and, with everyone's support, we will have another successful campaign this year. Our goal is to achieve contributions in excess of $1,350,000 and increase employee participation.
>
> I encourage each of your to give thoughtful consideration to contributing through the CFC. Let's work together to make life easier for our fellow Americans who are less fortunate.

3. Write a one-page memo to your supervisor at work (or to a potential supervisor in a potential, but real, job) requesting organizational funding for your Writing for Managers course. Provide justification focused on the value to the organization from this investment in funding.

4. You have a morale problem in your branch that has caused an attrition rate 25 percent higher than any other branch. The problem is that your boss (Joe Jones), who micromanages, has never met anyone deserving of an outstanding performance rating and constantly finds ways to criticize every employee for some shortcoming. The office has an Employee Recognition Program instituted two years ago by CEO Bill Moss, and the other three branches make ample use of it. Their production rates are two to three times what your branch manages each quarter. Select a decision maker and suggest a change that will improve morale and increase retention, but not get you fired.

5. Describe in a memorandum to your teacher a problem that occurred for you when you wrote or received a message, memorandum, letter, or report written in writer-centered language rather than reader-centered.

CHAPTER 3

Career Communication

A. Writing job descriptions and interviewing prospective employees

B. Performance assessments and the organization's goals

C. Providing evidence to support appraisals

D. Writing performance improvement plans

E. Writing recommendations

Managerial writing includes a large body of tasks that shape the future of the organization by defining its interaction with those to be hired and those employed. Employee performance goals and feedback are critical parts of this fabric, as are laying out expectations for employees in advance and finding the potential employee with the right fit for a specific position. When an employee moves on, the manager often is called upon to provide a promotion board, selection board, or a potential employer with an endorsement. All of the writing associated with these responsibilities must be accurate, complete, and carefully crafted.

A. Writing Job Descriptions and Interviewing Prospective Employees

The most costly part of an organization's expenses is the money required to hire, train, and keep employees on the payroll. In difficult economic times, companies downsize or "right-size" their work force, seek ways to make production more efficient (lean manufacturing and Six Sigma principles have proven attractive management devices recently), and remove middle layers of management so that workers can become "team leaders." Team leaders are responsible for organizing their portion of the workforce, supervising their co-workers' efforts, but do not have hiring or firing ability.

In the United States, between December 2007 and December 2010, according to the Economic Policy Institute (based on information from Bureau of Labor Statistics data), over 13 million employees lost their jobs and either got no replacement position or became underemployed in low-paying or part-time work (http://www.epi.org/publications/entry/jobs_picture_20100108/). With this reduction in size, the average company consolidated tasks once performed by a number of employees and assigned them to an employee remaining in the work force. Often, such assignments were not accompanied by an increase in pay, and less frequently, the posted job description did not change. Further, when overworked employees quit, new ones were hired at lower salaries and expected to do two to three times the number of tasks their predecessors were hired to do before the "right-sizing." As a consequence, potential and current employees are quite sensitive about what duties are expected and how employees are evaluated.

The job description is central to efficiency in management. In large organizations, the Human Resources Department will interview the manager, define the tasks to be assigned to each individual, and construct a job description for each position. In smaller organizations, these steps are the manager's task. The organization's ability to perform its mission and reach its production goals depends upon all tasks being defined, expectations being set for each employee, and uniform consequences being set out for employee failure to perform.

Here is a first step: listing the duties of the position.

Office Manager Job Description

Key Duties (This position is directly under the CEO)

1. Supervise the review, sorting, prioritization, and tagging of all incoming correspondence.
2. Supervise the creation of a suspense date for every piece of correspondence requiring action.
3. Ensure the tracking of suspense dates and ensure timely adherence.
4. Maintain filing system on incoming and outgoing correspondence.
5. Control use of conference area.
6. Set up all conferences, including seating, refreshments, writing materials, invitations, parking, and media requirements, including teleconferencing and phone connections.
7. Order, stock, inventory, and distribute all office supplies.
8. Monitor use and maintenance of copy machine, facsimile machine, electric stapler, postage machine, and all other office equipment.
9. Oversee maintenance of computers, intranet, and software/hardware acquisition, installation, and upgrade schedules.
10. Supervise office staff, evaluating performance, recommending for promotion, and providing any necessary disciplinary action.
11. Contract for office cleaning, furniture repair/purchase, and environmental safety.
12. Maintain, replace, add, or delete telephones and adjust billing as required.
13. Supervise client billing and payment of incoming bills, maintaining a suspense (deadline) system to ensure lateness avoidance.

continued

> 14. Arrange travel, accommodations, rental cars, and other related travel expenses for staff.
>
> 15. Prepare and submit a monthly status report to the CEO regarding these duties and any issues requiring executive-level decision.

To this basic list, a more detailed statement of expectations or standards of performance can be added.

It is the manager's obligation to review each job description for his or her employees on a regular basis and to incorporate any changes that might have occurred, in consultation with the affected employee. The employee's performance evaluation and continued employment depend on meeting the organization's expectations. Serious ramifications (with legal consequences) will occur if the duties change and the employee is not informed and thus fails to perform satisfactorily. Consider the job description as a contract that is in constant, ongoing revision with each employee. That is exactly what the job description is.

Interviewing Prospective Employees

There are three steps a manager must go through to select a low-risk, high-expectation individual to fill a job opening: (1) craft a job announcement that captures the essence of the job—describing each duty in priority order, (2) review the résumé and application letter of each candidate carefully, and (3) ask the "right" questions and look for the "right" body language and responses during a face-to-face interview.

How to Develop a Response to a Job Announcement

In recent years, the nature of the application for employment has changed dramatically. In addition to the explosion of media possibilities, resulting in electronic résumé formats, web-based forms, and the merger of the résumé with the cover letter to produce a single-page composite with two or three "bullets" and the required contact information, some portions of the printed résumé have been driven into extinction. For example, it is a dangerous practice to list a career objective today. Companies want an employee for a specific job, and a candidate who appears too ambitious (or one who states that the job will train him or her for something better) will have the résumé tossed in the trash can before another line is read—so say dozens of human resources (HR) professionals. Another entry that adds nothing and shows that the writer has copied a canned presentation is the phrase "References available upon request." Of course they are! Applicants using this phrase annoy harried gatekeepers who are reviewing hundreds of applications under extreme time constraints.

The following résumé is an example written by an imaginary Sara Jane Sprightly. She wants a bit more excitement in her life, although you can tell that she is well on her way to a rewarding career as an investment analyst. She spots an ad for an administrative support assistant in the Intelligence Community. She thinks that such a job would be challenging and exciting. Although the ad does not require any foreign language, Sara decided to add her own substantial expertise to the résumé because the popular image of the intelligence community involves language expertise.

What follows is her generic résumé, a composite ad for a fictitious job (based on a number of real job ads offered by all of the military services), an analysis of what the folks offering the position really want to see in a résumé, and a revision to Sara's résumé that addresses these particular needs. The revised result will most likely get Sara an interview, even though she is lacking some of the desired skills. Look for the subtleties as you read—not all are discussed, but *all* are important. Note, for example, that Sara's "stock" résumé is quite good, but most likely not good enough to get her the job. The difference lies mainly in the contents of the Qualification Summary, before and after she sees *and analyzes* (her professed skill) the want ad.

Sara Jane Sprightly **1625 Nomad Court** **301-555-1432 cell**
Pleasantville, MD 20201 **SJSprightly@comcast.net**
Fluent in Mandarin Chinese

QUALIFICATION SUMMARY

- Outstanding performance appraisals for past five years
- Rated top assistant analyst in division past two years
- Help customers make investment decisions
- Handled large sums as teller, more as loan officer
- Helped locals with quality of life issues on service mission
- Manage multiple suspenses easily

EXPERIENCE

Assistant Market Analyst, T. Rowe Price, Baltimore, MD 2008-Present

Provided guidance on investment planning, asset allocation, college funding, and retirement planning to 22 clients, resulted in company rating as top assistant analyst 2009, 2010, and doubling client assignment.

Assistant Financial Planner, First Federal Credit Union, Glen Burnie, MD 2005–2008

Began as teller, promoted to loan officer, then assistant financial planner, servicing 250 customers with their investment and estate planning. As teller routinely handled over $550,000 in error-free transactions weekly. As loan officer settled over $15 million in car and home transactions accurately, receiving $3,800 in bonuses and cash awards.

continued

Volunteer Service Mission, Hong Kong, China 2003–2005

Two-year volunteer service in Hong Kong, China, at own expense resulting in training and supervision of 16 volunteers, direct contact with over 70,000 nationals and indirect contact with over one million others (total immersion in language and culture), working to improve their quality of life. Received letter of commendation from high-ranking organization executive for scope and value of service.

OTHER EXPERIENCE

Cub Scout Den Leader, Pack 7670, Boy Scouts of America 2008–Present

Wood Badge graduate (Scouting's premier management training course), supervisor of two Assistant Den Leaders, guide for the growth and development of eight boys. Den has highest advancement record in the Pack, and has received many group and individual honors at area and local contests and competitions. Recognized for service as recipient of District Award of Merit.

EDUCATION AND TRAINING

Bachelor of Science, Financial Management (Minor: Chinese), Utah State University 2003

Magna Cum Laude, Phi Beta Kappa, Who's Who Among Students in Colleges and Universities
One year overseas study, East China University of Science and Technology, Shanghai (2001-Fellowship)

Wood Badge (Boy Scout Senior Management Course) 2010

BUILDING A QUALIFICATION SUMMARY

CAPTURING THE REQUIREMENTS

Copy the requirements portion of the ad into a word processing file:

Administrative Support Assistant, US Air Force Air Intelligence Agency (AIA), 70th Intelligence Wing, Fort Meade, MD

This is a civilian, Government-Grade Excepted (GGE) appointment within the Department of Defense, US Air Force Air Combat Command. The incumbent will research/obtain background information for required actions using automated databases/historical files/review previous or current studies/projects. Assist/advise

continued

staff/action officers on procedural/administrative aspects of staff actions. Review/ evaluate special projects/action papers ensuring appropriate coordination has been effected; procedural requirements met; style/composition/grammar is correct/ security markings are correctly applied, ensuring compliance with regulatory guidance. Assist with creation of civilian personnel actions/policies; coordinate/ accomplish civilian personnel actions for employees to include but not limited to appointments, promotions, reassignments, etc. Assist with execution ensuring funds of the assigned segment of the budget (credit cards, training, and yearly agency supplies). Manage operating schedule/long-range calendar of Senior Advisor, Chief Division/staff. Prepare/coordinate travel orders/agendas; correspondence/office supplies/equipment.

QUALIFICATIONS REQUIRED

- Specialized experience is experience with administrative concepts, procedures and practices evaluating clerical and administrative procedures, grammar, sentence structure and punctuation, creating spreadsheets, databases, tracking suspenses and preparing reports or summaries on specific actions, and preparing travel arrangement.

- At a minimum, your résumé must reflect one year of demonstrated experience performing the duties listed above (specialized experience) which must be comparable to the next lower GGE/Band. You must document that you have a current successful performance evaluation.

- Applicants claiming Veterans Preference must submit required paperwork at time of selection.

- CONDITIONS OF EMPLOYMENT: All AIA employees may be subject to extended temporary duty (TDY) or worldwide deployments during crisis situations to perform mission essential functions as determined by management.

- Must be able to obtain and maintain a TOP SECRET security clearance based on a single scope background investigation (SSBI) with eligibility for sensitive compartmented information (SCI).

- In accordance with Air Force Instruction 36-810, Substance Abuse Prevention and Control, the incumbent of this position must successfully pass a urinalysis screening for illegal drug use prior to appointment and periodically thereafter.

- Must be willing to undergo and successfully complete a counterintelligence-scope polygraph examination with No Deception Indicated (NDI) on a pre-appointment and periodic basis.

Creating a List

Do so by pressing the Return or Enter key twice after each separate requirement in the listing you copied into your file. This creates a list that you can then number and address, one item at a time:

1. Will research/obtain background information for required actions using automated databases/historical files/review previous or current studies/projects.

2. Assist/advise staff/action officers on procedural/administrative aspects of staff actions.

3. Review/evaluate special projects/action papers ensuring appropriate coordination has been effected; procedural requirements met; style/composition/grammar is correct/security markings are correctly applied, ensuring compliance with regulatory guidance.

4. Assist with creation of civilian personnel actions/policies; coordinate/accomplish civilian personnel actions for employees to include but not limited to appointments, promotions, reassignments, etc.

5. Assist with execution ensuring funds of the assigned segment of the budget (credit cards, training, and yearly agency supplies).

6. Manage operating schedule/long-range calendar of Senior Advisor, Chief Division/staff.

7. Prepare/coordinate travel orders/agendas; correspondence/office supplies/equipment.

8. Specialized experience is experience with administrative concepts, procedures and practices evaluating clerical and administrative procedures, grammar, sentence structure and punctuation, creating spreadsheets, databases, tracking suspenses and preparing reports or summaries on specific actions, and preparing travel arrangement.

9. At a minimum, your résumé must reflect one year of demonstrated experience performing the duties listed above (specialized experience) which must be comparable to the next lower GGE/Band. You must document that you have a current successful performance evaluation.

10. Applicants claiming Veterans Preference must submit required paperwork at time of selection.

11. All AIA employees may be subject to extended temporary duty (TDY) or worldwide deployments during crisis situations to perform mission essential functions as determined by management.

12. Must be able to obtain and maintain a TOP SECRET security clearance based on a single scope background investigation (SSBI) with eligibility for sensitive compartmented information (SCI).

13. In accordance with Air Force Instruction 36-810, Substance Abuse Prevention and Control, the incumbent of this position must successfully pass a urinalysis screening for illegal drug use prior to appointment and periodically thereafter.

14. Must be willing to undergo and successfully complete a counterintelligence-scope polygraph examination with No Deception Indicated (NDI) on a pre-appointment and periodic basis.

Prioritizing and Grouping the List

Look for repeated requirements (a strong indication that the ad was written by several people and that the repeated item is high on the list of key items for the successful candidate to be able to do).

1. Must be able to obtain and maintain a TOP SECRET security clearance based on a single scope background investigation (SSBI) with eligibility for sensitive compartmented information (SCI).

2. Must be willing to undergo and successfully complete a counterintelligence-scope polygraph examination with No Deception Indicated (NDI) on a pre-appointment and periodic basis.

3. Specialized experience is experience with administrative concepts, procedures and practices evaluating clerical and administrative procedures, grammar, sentence structure and punctuation, creating spreadsheets, databases, tracking suspenses and preparing reports or summaries on specific actions, and preparing travel arrangement.

4. At a minimum, your resume must reflect one year of demonstrated experience performing the duties listed below (specialized experience) which must be comparable to the next lower GGE/Band. You must document that you have a current successful performance evaluation.

    a. Will research/obtain background information for required actions using automated databases/historical files/review previous or current studies/projects.

    b. Assist/advise staff/action officers on procedural/administrative aspects of staff actions.

    c. Review/evaluate special projects/action papers ensuring appropriate coordination has been effected; procedural requirements met; style/composition/grammar is correct/security markings are correctly applied ensuring compliance with regulatory guidance.

    d. Assist with creation of civilian personnel actions/policies; coordinate/accomplish civilian personnel actions for employees to include but not limited to appointments, promotions, reassignments, etc.

    e. Assist with execution ensuring funds of the assigned segment of the budget (credit cards, training, and yearly agency supplies).

    f. Manage operating schedule/long-range calendar of Senior Advisor, Chief Division/staff.

    g. Prepare/coordinate travel orders/agendas; correspondence/office supplies/equipment.

The following need not be addressed in a qualification summary:

5.   Applicants claiming Veterans Preference must submit required paperwork at time of selection.

6.   All INSCOM employees may be subject to extended temporary duty (TDY) or worldwide deployments during crisis situations to perform mission essential functions as determined by management.

7.   Air Force Instruction 36-810, Substance Abuse Prevention and Control, the incumbent of this position must successfully pass a urinalysis screening for illegal drug use prior to appointment and periodically thereafter.

Compare the resulting requirement list with the existing qualification summary and make the necessary changes.

Requirements

1.   Must be able to obtain and maintain a TOP SECRET security clearance based on a single scope background investigation (SSBI) with eligibility for sensitive compartmented information (SCI).

2.   Must be willing to undergo and successfully complete a counterintelligence-scope polygraph examination with No Deception Indicated (NDI) on a pre-appointment and periodic basis.

3.   Specialized experience is experience with administrative concepts, procedures and practices evaluating clerical and administrative procedures, grammar, sentence structure and punctuation, creating spreadsheets, databases, tracking suspenses and preparing reports or summaries on specific actions, and preparing travel arrangement.

4.   At a minimum, your résumé must reflect one year of demonstrated experience performing the duties listed below (specialized experience) which must be comparable to the next lower GGE/Band. You must document that you have a current successful performance evaluation.

   a.   Will research/obtain background information for required actions using automated databases/historical files/review previous or current studies/projects.

   b.   Assist/advise staff/action officers on procedural/administrative aspects of staff actions.

   c.   Review/evaluate special projects/action papers ensuring appropriate coordination has been effected; procedural requirements met; style/composition/grammar is correct/security markings are correctly applied ensuring compliance with regulatory guidance.

   d.   Assist with creation of civilian personnel actions/policies; coordinate/accomplish civilian personnel actions for employees to include but not limited to appointments, promotions, reassignments, etc.

e.   Assist with execution ensuring funds of the assigned segment of the budget (credit cards, training, and yearly agency supplies).

f.   Manage operating schedule/long-range calendar of Senior Advisor, Chief Division/staff.

g.   Prepare/coordinate travel orders/agendas; correspondence/office supplies/equipment.

Existing Qualification Summary

- Outstanding performance appraisals for past five years
- Rated top assistant analyst in division past two years
- Help customers make investment decisions
- Handled large sums as teller, more as loan officer
- Helped locals with quality of life issues on service mission
- Manage multiple suspenses easily

REVISED RÉSUMÉ

Sara Jane Sprightly	**1625 Nomad Court** **Pleasantville, MD 20201**	**301-555-1432 cell** SJSprightly@comcast.net

Current FBI Background Check (BSA Leader)

Fluent in Mandarin Chinese

"Sara is one of the most exceptional analysts I have seen in 20 years as a supervisor."

—Clara Snedley, T. Rowe Price

QUALIFICATION SUMMARY

- Outstanding performance appraisals for past five years
- Rated top assistant analyst in division past two years
- Routinely prepared time-sensitive, error-free contractual documents for million-dollar account transactions, earning thousands of dollars in bonuses for attention to detail
- Chinese fluency obtained from four years of college training plus three years in-country learning culture and customs
- Daily creation, population, and manipulation of complex spreadsheets in Excel and Quattro Pro, tracking multiple suspenses and never missing a deadline

continued

- Daily, detailed research of investment trends, comprehensive analysis, advising seniors and clients on transactions often over $1 million, with consistently accurate results

EXPERIENCE

Assistant Market Analyst, T. Rowe Price, Baltimore, MD 2008–Present

Provided guidance on investment planning, asset allocation, college funding, and retirement planning to 22 clients, resulted in company rating as top assistant analyst 2009, 2010, and doubling client assignment.

Assistant Financial Planner, First Federal Credit Union, Glen Burnie, MD 2005–2008

Began as teller, promoted to loan officer, then assistant financial planner, servicing 250 customers with their investment and estate planning. As teller, routinely handled over $550,000 in error-free transactions weekly. As loan officer, settled over $15 million in car and home transactions accurately, receiving $3,800 in bonuses and cash awards.

Volunteer Service Mission, Hong Kong, China 2003–2005

Two-year volunteer service in Hong Kong, China, at own expense, resulting in training and supervision of 16 volunteers, direct contact with over 70,000 nationals, and indirect contact with over one million others (total immersion in language and culture), working to improve their quality of life. Received letter of commendation from high-ranking organization executive for scope and value of service.

OTHER EXPERIENCE

Cub Scout Den Leader, Pack 7670, Boy Scouts of America 2008–Present

Wood Badge graduate (Scouting's premier management training course), supervisor of two Assistant Den Leaders, guide for the growth and development of eight boys. Den has highest advancement record in the Pack and has received many group and individual honors at area and local contests and competitions. Recognized for service as recipient of District Award of Merit.

EDUCATION AND TRAINING

Bachelor of Science, Financial Management (Minor: Chinese), Utah State University 2003

Magna cum laude, Phi Beta Kappa, Who's Who Among Students in Colleges and Universities

One year overseas study, East China University of Science and Technology, Shanghai (2001 Fellowship)

Wood Badge, (Boy Scout Senior Management Course) 2010

How the Modification Improved the Résumé

Note that the Qualification entries have now been adjusted, information concerning her clearance status has been included, and information about her language- and detail-oriented clerical capabilities have been expanded to be *specific*. What management wants to see in such a résumé is this simple formula repeated over and over again: *claim* + *example* (including quantity and scope) + *results*. Not also that Sara has added her clearance status—important not only because clearances are costly, but also because having passed the FBI background check is a significant first step and will put her ahead of many other applicants. Note also the inclusion of a testimonial. This one-line praise from a supervisor addresses her most significant attribute as *observed* and reduces the potential employer's risk significantly.

The top third of the first page of a résumé is often the only thing read during an initial screening, and now Sara's résumé includes her language, clearance, and analytic skills up front, plus six *key* attributes with scope/quantity and results in a Qualification Summary—all on the top third of the page.

Reviewing Résumés and Cover Letters

Most job application materials are reviewed initially through automated key word search software or by a manual screening. The manual screening results in three piles: forget it, maybe, and Wow! Questions to ask in the mechanical review:

1. Does the résumé reflect applicant understanding of the specific job offered and has he or she tailored the résumé accordingly? (A generic résumé indicates that the candidate is not likely to be conscientious or pay enough attention to detail to be a good risk.)

2. Does the Qualification Summary show a low risk to our organization because the applicant has had the appropriate recognition for quality performance elsewhere, in the form of a number of promotions, salary increases, and other achievements?

3. Are the applicant's achievements substantive and do they reflect initiative and analytic capability that will transfer to our organization?

4. Are the candidate's Experience section entries complete with quantities, scope, and results?

5. Does a scan of Facebook, MySpace, and other electronic social media reflect any negative traits (such as negative comments about employers or a focus on drinking or other activity not desirable for our employees)?

6. Did the applicant employ "trick" efforts, such as including multiple typed entries of key search terms in a white color so the computer will count them but a visual review will not reveal the needless repetition? This is a sure sign of candidate incompetence and reliance on something other than proven worth to earn a favorable decision.

The Face-to-Face Interview

Copyright © by Bob Thaves. Reprinted by permission of United Media.

As this *Frank & Ernest* cartoon suggests, the potential employee who demonstrates that he or she does not understand the company's focus and needs should not be selected for the empty position.

During the face-to-face interview, many candidates will be nervous. Many have been out of work for months (the national average during 2010 was six months, according to the Bureau of Labor Statistics). Obviously, they will have gaps in employment, and many will have bad credit ratings. The *first* thing the manager must do is put the candidate at ease. There are certain questions the manager cannot ask a candidate (see Chapter 6) and others that are "standard fare" for most interviews. The questions you ask should reveal to you the candidate's risk level as a new employee. Ask what the candidate perceives his or her biggest weakness to be, how he or she got along with the previous employer, why he or she left, and what he or she thinks is the greatest asset he or she will bring to this organization if hired. Watch for body language, but remember that cultural differences transmit differently. For example, a potential employee from an Eastern culture may not wish to look you in the eye because of your elevated position—to do so would be disrespectful. Some cultures put great stock in unceasing hand gestures; others do not. Do *not* make a judgment without understanding the *reason* for the response and what it represents.

B. Performance Assessments and the Organization's Goals

How well or how poorly an employee performs is measured by the organization's goals and by the defined tasks the employee is expected to perform in a specific position. Some organizations fail to measure employee performance and the result inevitably is inefficiencies in organizational and individual production. The old adage "Fail to plan and you plan to fail" has merit and application here.

Performance assessment tools are many and come in a large variety of formats. All, however, focus on two aspects of employee performance: (1) how well the employee performed in the past (usually a set period such as a year, half-year, or quarter-year), and (2) the employee's future potential for promotion or increased responsibility.

The format can be blocks to check, blocks with a ten-word-or-less/more description of a highlight, a narrative, or "bullets" (nonsentence statements of accomplishments or shortcomings). Written assessments should contain three elements: (1) a description of some duty or achievement or failure, (2) the scope or quantity of the event or situation, and (3) the impact. So, if Roger was your top salesperson last quarter, you do Roger a disservice by merely writing, "Roger was our top salesperson this quarter." Instead, describe the achievement by noting that "Roger was top in sales, exceeding his personal goal by 97 percent and increasing sales revenues for the entire division by 18 percent. He earned a 10 percent salary bonus as a result."

Likewise, if Roger was a disappointment, don't just note, "Roger continues to display poor customer relations despite counseling and has not attended the required people skills training." Write instead, "Roger continues to have problems with customer relations as evidenced by 15 customer complaints and a 5 percent decline in repeat sales to his customers. He has failed to attend three required people skills classes and has been formally counseled on four occasions during the period." Omitting the detail and the evidence will permit Roger to appeal an adverse evaluation ("Roger displays poor people skills") as being your personal bias and an unsubstantiated claim. Quite likely, a review board would strike the unfavorable comments and Roger would be well on his way to an undeserved promotion.

Evaluations should assess future potential, and that assessment should be based on specific achievements with their scope or quantity and their impact. The evaluation is part of a "paper trail" of performance attributes that allows a promotion board to measure achievement and potential against all others in the same pay grade and make defensible decisions regarding those deserving of promotion and why. In the small organization, the manager himself or herself is the promotion board and the evaluations are the documentation that provides the justification for manager action if the decision is ever challenged by an employee or by upper-level management.

Record keeping is a critical part of a manager's ability to assess performance. However, there are legal restrictions governing the type and content of records a manager can keep on an employee. A cardinal rule is *never* keep notes expressing unsupported, *personal* opinion, such as "Fred continues to be as lazy as before." See Chapter 6 for a further discussion of the limitations involved.

Organizational Goals and Evaluations

If Roger performs well in relation to assigned tasks, and if those tasks have resulted from a job description that mirrors the organization's mission and goals, then "all is right with the world" (Robert Browning, "Pippa Passes"). Expectations *must* be realistic and must be based on the organization mission and goals before what employees actually *do* on the job fully support what needs to be done. See Chapter 6 for a discussion of how to develop effective mission and vision statements and the strategic planning that makes them come to pass.

C. Providing Evidence to Support Appraisals

An appraisal without evidence is a series of personal opinions and empty claims, subject to appeal by the employee, challenge by a promotion or review board, and of absolutely no value as an assessment tool. Evidence provided in *effective* appraisals comes from a variety of sources: work logs, notes to the supervisor, interim reports, outgoing correspondence, notes and assessments from customers and other organizations, daily notes kept by the manager, or periodic assessment meetings between the manager and the employee.

If Roger developed a Procedural Guide during the evaluation period, that is something you should mention in his appraisal. But how was this task related to his duties of supporting customers and solving technical problems? The relationship must be clear in your written evaluation. Now consider that this guide helped his peers solve technological problems faster, thus serving customers more accurately and faster. Good—that is the link you need to connect this achievement with his job description. But one question remains: what were the results of this task? Suppose the results were that all telephone calls for incidents since the guide had been distributed now take two-thirds the time to resolve. Merely stating in the appraisal that "Roger developed a guide that permitted his division to resolve trouble calls more rapidly" would be a disservice to Roger and a poor statement of what actually happened. Roger also implemented the guide, and the results were significant. What really happened was, "Roger developed and implemented a guide that reduced the division troubleshooting time by two-thirds." This comment is an effective use of the evidence you have as a manager that Roger has been effective in performing his duties.

The content of a performance appraisal assessment should never come as a surprise to an employee.

D. Writing Performance Improvement Plans

Not all employees exceed expectations all the time, and many do not even *meet* all expectations all of the time. This fact of management requires the manager to take steps to improve individual employee performance. For those employees whose performance does not improve, no matter what the manager does, there must be some sort of documentation to support the decision to discipline or dismiss the employee. This vehicle—one that documents failure, improvement goals, and either the achievement of those goals or the continued failure to achieve them—is a *performance improvement plan*.

Performance goals *must* be tied to a job description that addresses the organization's mission and goals or it will be successfully challenged as arbitrary and capricious. There are many formats for a performance goals contract, but all have in common the following:

1. A list of areas for improvement
2. A list of specific actions required to address each area marked as needing improvement

3. A timetable for actions to be completed

4. A signature section to be signed and dated by the employee and by the manager

If employee performance is below an acceptable level, the manager should notify the employee in writing (see http://www.nps.gov/training/tel/guides/pip_guide_080707.pdf) that he or she has an "opportunity to improve" and invite the employee to a meeting at which a specific plan will be developed.

Keep in mind that there are many reasons for poor performance. Among them are not understanding the task, having a physical or mental issue that prohibits conformance, or having a negative attitude toward the work or the supervisor.

If physical or mental issues are present, the employee is protected by law and the manager has specific responsibilities (see Chapter 6 for more discussion on this topic) regarding how to handle the situation. For example, if the employee has developed a sudden, severe, and permanent hearing loss, then the manager has a specific responsibility to adjust the employee's work to accommodate the disability. However, if the job requires hearing, then the remedy is to transfer the employee. If that is not possible, then medical retirement may be the only option.

Below-standard performance might result in performance actions (the Performance Improvement Plan being a key element) or, in some cases, disciplinary action. The organization should have written policy that addresses both options, and these guidelines should have been reviewed for legality and completeness well before the issue requiring the meeting between this manager and this employee occurs.

E. Writing Recommendations

A pleasant but demanding task is the responsibility of a manager to write a recommendation for an employee. The recommendation might be for the employee to receive an award, be favorably considered for a special assignment, or to be considered for a school or following employment opportunity.

Whatever the occasion, the employer should carefully review the specific requirements to be addressed in the recommendation, including the preferred format, content, and address components.

Writing a recommendation requires reliance on documentation; care in reporting accomplishments with quantities, scope, and results; and focus on the requirements to be met—the same components required in constructing a performance appraisal. In writing an assessment for an employee to be favorably considered for an award or educational opportunity, the manager must be specific in describing his or her own personal qualifications (credibility) to make the recommendation.

Summary

In this chapter, we have examined how to write job descriptions and interview prospective employees, develop performance assessments that match the organization's goals, provide evidence to support appraisals, write performance improvement plans, and write recommendations.

The job description is a dynamic instrument that reflects *current* duties and should be discussed with the incumbent employee often, especially when *any* alteration is contemplated or made.

Résumés and job application correspondence should be reviewed by the hiring manager for (1) relevance to the position advertised, (2) the potential employee's past promotions and achievements as indicators of probable performance with our organization, and (3) the presence of any "tricks" such as scannable repeated keywords, border art, and any other indicator that the applicant is hiding a lack of substance.

The job interview should determine the risk of hiring a specific individual and that individual's proven potential to do the specific job. Ask questions that draw out the candidate's past accomplishments, attitude, demonstrated initiative, and understanding of past employment and what the current position offered entails.

Performance assessments *must* be governed by the organization mission and functions to be appropriate. Their content must include specific, documented examples to be effective. The content of such assessments *never* should come as a surprise to the employee.

Writing both performance improvement plans and recommendations require the writer to use specific examples, quantify them, and explain the results of the employee's actions or required actions.

SUGGESTED ASSIGNMENTS

1. Write Bill Blizzard's annual performance review. Use a narrative, third-person ("Bill or Mr. Blizzard did so-and-so," *not* "You did so-and-so") format with the five headings specified in the following list. Remember to keep the appraisal balanced. Include his specific contributions to the mission, strengths, areas in need of attention, recommendations for improvement, and potential for promotion. You may consider the following wording as your own notes, so copying appropriate portions for this assignment will *not* be considered plagiarism.

Background

You are the manager of the Client Support Division at Crystar Enterprises, a computer software firm in Columbia, Maryland. One of your people, Bill Blizzard, a client support specialist, has been with the firm and your division for one year and you are required to prepare his annual performance review. At Crystar, such reviews follow a narrative, third-person format with sections for **ACCOMPLISHMENTS, STRENGTHS, AREAS NEEDING IMPROVEMENT, SPECIFIC RECOMMENDATIONS FOR IMPROVEMENT** (guidance as to what action the employee can take to better fulfill the needs of the position and the company), and **PROMOTION POTENTIAL**.

Bill is a 28-year-old technical specialist with six years of computer experience, including the year with your division. Because of restructuring within Crystar almost immediately after his arrival, Bill has had to handle more general customer support as well as technical problems. Bill is outstanding (for his experience level) in his technical skills, and has a good "track record" as a troubleshooter. Specifically, he developed a new troubleshooting procedure guide that lets less-experienced workers spot problems and solve them in less than a third of the time required previously. In the past year, Bill has solved over 100 serious client application problems, winning repeat business and sound customer relations with clients having large accounts. However, Bill's people skills remain marginal, despite specific discussions and goal-setting sessions you have had with him each quarter of the past year. He attended one sensitivity training class (one week) during the second quarter, but has made excuses for not attending the additional people skills seminars you recommended in the last two quarterly reviews. Bill tends to become frustrated when dealing with problems that he feels clients should be able to solve on their own. His attitude shows through when dealing with those clients; he is frequently brusque and impatient with nontechnical clients, many of who have complained to you about what they perceive as his arrogance.

You hired Bill because of his technical skills and his potential to be groomed as a Client Technical Support Branch manager, but you have been a bit disappointed in the lack of flexibility he has shown so far. You still feel that Bill has high potential, but that he will need to redirect his priorities if he is to meet your expectations of him.

Bill has strong organizational skills and is very good at time management. In some ways, his attempts at efficiency may be alienating clients. He tends to want problems defined precisely so he can diagnose them and resolve them quickly and efficiently. Several nontechnical clients have explained problems in such general terms that Bill has lost his patience and voiced his frustration plainly.

Crystar is committed to excellent client support, but must use its downsized, limited resources wisely. Bill understands the company's commitment and has tried to separate genuine problems (those caused by defects in the product) from user-created problems caused by their particular application or "customization" of the software or their computer "illiteracy." His attempt to control costs has alienated some clients who have threatened to seek other vendors unless they have better support from Crystar. They have complained about his lack of responsiveness and his unwillingness to solve what they perceive to be shortcomings in the software.

Write Bill's performance review. Add any details you think appropriate but *don't change the basic situation*. Provide specific guidance as to what Bill might do to improve his performance and fulfill the potential you see in him. Bill thinks he has been doing a conscientious job and will be surprised by any negative comments in his review. To upset him might mean his resignation. However, despite three quarterly reviews, Bill has continued to concentrate on the areas of his technical expertise rather than developing the broader managerial and supervisory skills the company needs. Instead of delegating major tasks, he has tried to solve all really challenging problems himself. He needs to learn how to delegate responsibility and to oversee those who must carry out routine tasks.

2. Write the Job Description for Bill Blizzard *after* the downsizing described in assignment 1.

3. Write a Performance Improvement Plan for Bill. Noting that Bill has not profited by attending (or avoiding) people skills training and that your goal is to change Bill's performance, task him with creating and implementing a Customer Troubleshooting Guide that will eliminate much of the customer behavior that Bill cannot deal with and explain *why* Bill should perform this task.

4. Write a Letter of Recommendation for Bill after he opts to leave the company rather than deal with customers he cannot tolerate. Be truthful, but remember that laws protect Bill from some negative things you might wish to say.

5. Select an actual ad for a job you would like to have. Produce a one-page analysis of the ad and generate a résumé addressing the key requirements in your qualification summary. Package the result as the résumé followed by your ad assessment, with a copy of the ad attached as the last page(s).

Treat the words of this assignment as YOUR personal notes; consequently, copying sentences or phrasing into your paper will NOT be plagiarism.

CHAPTER 4

Managerial Reporting and Proposal Writing

    A.   Selecting appropriate report and proposal formats; customizing formats

    B.   Planning complex reports

    C.   Evaluating and presenting qualitative and quantitative information

    D.   Visual information and presentations

    E.   Sample researched proposal

A. Selecting Appropriate Report and Proposal Formats; Customizing Formats

Managerial reports and proposals serve two major purposes: to inform or to persuade. However, when you consider that most informational reports are provided to become the basis for managerial decisions, then it is safe to state that *all* managerial reporting and proposal writing has some foundation in presenting to persuade.

Most organizations have a set of standardized formats for specific reports and each organization differs in presentation requirements to a certain degree, so this chapter will focus on the *common* elements of reports and proposals—and *why* they are present. The distinction between a report and a proposal is somewhat vague: *proposals* request action and seek to persuade a decision maker to take that action; *reports* tell of events and statuses, but often ask for action or are presented in response to a management request so that action can be taken on what is reported.

A stockholders' report, for example, may be quite lengthy (100 pages or more) or very short—often only one page printed in color front and back and containing pie and bar charts, tables, and other visual devises (examined later in this chapter) as well as words to report to stockholders what happened in the past year and what is proposed for the next year. On occasion, these short reports take the form of a single sheet folded in thirds and read as a pamphlet.

One of the shortest, and most powerful, managerial reports on record was sent by Julius Caesar to the Senate of Rome in May of 47 BC after he defeated Pharnaces II near the town of Zela (where Pharnace's father, Mithridates IV, had defeated the Romans 20 years before): "Veni, vidi, vici" ("I came, I saw, I conquered") (http://www.unrv.com/fall-republic/veni-vidi-vici.php).

All reports and proposals have in common the same ingredients you find in a memorandum: a SUBJECT, DATE, whom it is "TO and FROM names or titles," plus a BODY. Complex reports and proposals also have sections called Front Matter and Back Matter as add-ons to the core report.

Report or proposal generation begins with a consideration of *what* is to be told and *who* it is to be told to. Short reports are created to meet simple needs to persuade or inform. Those reports include status and activity reports, trip reports, short proposals, action summaries, and special-purpose documents created to meet one-time, specialized needs.

The key to information acceptance often is the selection of an appropriate format. A Position Paper, for example, will state, on one page, what you could expand to a three-page report. But, if time is of the essence and the decision is critical, the shorter form may be easier to absorb and comprehend. The key to report form selection is the answer to the questions: what does the recipient *expect*? What does the recipient *need*? What will make your case in the best, fail-safe way?

Many *formats* are available on the Web, packaged with your word processor, or in style manuals where you work. However, just because a format calls for a certain section does *not* mean that you *must* include that section.

In a résumé, for example (which is a persuasive proposal directed toward a specific decision maker), some formats call for a chronological listing of your experience. That format might bury relevant experience you had a year or so ago, but a functional résumé will not. Moreover, most formats call for a Career Objective section, but as the nation recovers from a deep-seated depression, most companies are *not* interested in your desires for growth and expanded responsibilities and they certainly are *not* interested in plans that carry you away from them at some critical point in your future. Don't use this section (except to specify a position job number for which you are applying, perhaps). This is a simple conclusion to reach if you stop to realize that the résumé, just like any other proposal, is *not* about *you*, but about what you can do for the decision maker.

Sample Short Report

DATE: July 8, 20xx
TO: Bob Preston
FROM: John Deavers
SUBJECT: Quarterly Report from Sales

The Sales Department is pleased to present our report for the Third Quarter 20xx.

continued

Introduction

Overall sales this quarter were up by 22 percent from previous quarter, largely due to the introduction of a new sales tracking software program, HELIX, which has made tracking the stages of sales initiatives instantly available throughout the department.

One area still needs attention: Government Contract Tracking. We have made this a top priority for the next quarter and have dedicated one staff member, Ralph Cartwright to the task of applying the HELIX tracking system to past sales to analyze what stages of the process require strengthening and what is working at an acceptable level.

Discussion

Because of HELIX, sales in five states (Maryland, Virginia, West Virginia, North Carolina, and South Carolina) increased by 37 percent this past quarter. This is attributed to the software picking up dropped offers that were being missed by our staff because of the sheer volume of business from our regional office covering these five states.

Government sales were our only disappointment during the quarter. Until the end of the quarter, our government sales were managed by the Regional Center in which they occurred. As a consequence, there was no one central point of contact monitoring this activity. Our initial run of the HELIX program identified a much larger percentage of incomplete transactions because of this management practice, so we have assigned Ralph Cartwright on our headquarters staff to oversee *all* government sales and also to research what stages in the process historically have resulted in errors. Regional offices will still directly manage government sales in their territories, but they will report the initiation of each sales process to Ralph, who will then track the transactions centrally via HELIX.

Conclusion

The HELIX program has proven a sound investment for this department. Our local staff and every member of every regional team has been with the company over five years, and their sustained contributions have been a solid growth factor for the company during that period. As the company grows, I feel confident that this new technology will continue to make our efforts bear fruit.

What value would a bar chart have in making the quarterly results more "visible"? Would a table with sales statistics from every region help or confuse the report? How about a picture of Ralph Cartwright? Would you put a cover sheet on this report? Why or why not? What would you expect Bob Preston's reaction to be? Considering the problem with tracking government sales, which—by inference—had gone on for more than just the past quarter, why do you suppose John Deavers included specific praise for the Sales staff and regional offices, to the extent of mentioning their loyal service for over five years? What message does this section send Bob Preston?

B. Planning Complex Reports

Complex reports and proposals take a little more planning than their shorter cousins. Such documents include a core report, but also include "Front Matter" and "Back Matter" sections. Typically, front matter will consist of (in this order): a Letter of Transmittal or a Routing Slip, a Title Page, an Executive Summary (technical reports also include an Abstract), a Table of Contents, and a List of Illustrations. The back matter includes a Works Cited page (for a business report or proposal, which use the non-time-sensitive, secondary source permissive MLA reference system) or a References page (for a technical or scientific product, which uses the APA reference system that includes the year of publication in the in-text citation and demands inclusion of primary sources only), a Glossary of Terms, and Appendices, as required.

Typically, the externals are completed *after* the core report or proposal has been produced; however, a good technique for assuring that the message is not lost somewhere in the lengthy report or proposal is to write a draft Executive Summary *first*. The Executive Summary contains a *summary* of the final report or proposal. If you write it first, you won't be distracted by difficulties that arise as you compose the extended version. This technique practically guarantees that you will not suffer writer's block when time is of the essence.

C. Evaluating and Presenting Qualitative and Quantitative Information

From *How to Lie with Statistics* by Darrell Huff illustrated by Irving Geis. Copyright 1954 and renewed © 1982 by Darrell Huff and Irving Geis. Used by permission of W.W. Norton & Company, Inc.

Format is critical to easy comprehension, but content is vital to ultimate understanding and action. Reports and proposals contain both qualitative and quantitative information— information that must be documented as accurate and complete, then presented in a way that helps the reader understand and react appropriately. Qualitative information consists of facts represented by words, photographs, film clips, or other visual devices; quantitative information consists of facts that can be represented by graphs and charts, tables, and other visual comparative devices.

In an article on "Types of Data" on the Web (Research Methods Knowledge Base, http://www. socialresearchmethods.net/kb/datatype.php), William Trochim notes:

> Personally, while I find the distinction between qualitative and quantitative data to have some utility, I think most people draw too hard a distinction, and that can lead to all sorts of confusion. In some areas of social research, the qualitative-quantitative distinction has led to protracted arguments with the proponents of each arguing the superiority of their kind of data over the other. The quantitative types argue that their data is "hard," "rigorous," "credible," and "scientific." The qualitative proponents counter that their data is "sensitive," "nuanced," "detailed," and "contextual."

There is an old saw, wrongly attributed as originating with Mark Twain, but actually much older, that "figures don't lie, but liars do figure." Well, the truth is that figures *can* be misconstrued, or poorly presented, or partially presented, with the result that they *do* lie. What is true of quantitative data is also the case with qualitative information. The managerial writer has to be exceptionally careful to present these anchors in context. In Shakespeare's *Macbeth* (Act 4, Scene i) the witches promise Macbeth that "none of woman born shall harm Macbeth." Although the statement is accurate, it is incomplete. Macbeth meets his death by the sword of Macduff, one taken by Caesarean section and "not of woman born."

D. Visual Information and Presentations

Graphs, charts, tables, drawings, and pictures display visually that which might take many words to render. There is an old saying that "one picture is worth a thousand words." People argue as to whether Napoleon first stated this, or an American, or whether the saying is indeed ancient Chinese, mistranslated from "one picture is worth ten thousand *characters*—the number of characters in the Chinese alphabet. Regardless, the obvious truth is that a photograph or a graphic can communicate a complex idea that a writer using many words might have difficulty with.

Certainly not a doctrinal rule, but a wise standard, is the advice to integrate all graphics on the page on which they are discussed. Many writers make adjustments to graphs and charts on stand-alone pages and then fail to correct the text that appears elsewhere (or vice versa, for that matter). Having text and graphic appear together lessens the chance that unilateral errors will cause confusion in the reader's mind as he or she relies on one or the other, perhaps without ever noticing the discrepancy or realizing that the one relied on is the one that has not been corrected.

E. Sample Researched Proposal

John Jenkins is an employee assigned to one of the four Production branches that work in shifts at Crystar in Columbia, Maryland. Each shift has 20 employees who copy, label, and package software discs in plastic containers called CD "jewel cases," in which they also insert printed covers with instructions. Crystar produces computer software used by major corporations in the United States and abroad. John has a major problem: his boss, Henry Purcell, is a micromanager who, in 30 years as a supervisor, has never met an outstanding worker. John's shift is the only one that must sign out to use the bathroom. Employee attrition on John's shift is twice that of the other shifts, production is two-thirds that of the other three shifts, and, although Crystar has a working Employee Recognition Program, no one on John's shift has received an award in the past 24 months, yet there are at least two such awards every month on the other shifts.

John wants to write a researched proposal that will change this circumstance, but he knows that Henry will go ballistic when he reads it and the repercussions on John will be unbearable. What should he do?

The Problem

John has a problem: a micromanaging, non-supportive boss. But that is *not* the problem that needs to be changed *from the company perspective*. The real problem from management's perspective is the high attrition rate and low production rate on John's shift. That circumstance would also be accompanied by a constant training effort that also detracts from production (an argument that Henry has used successfully when his boss, Susan Goforth, has questioned him on the consistently low production rate—Henry has to spend more time training workers than the other three shift managers do).

The Solution

It is obvious that proposing a change to Henry will not only fail to solve the problem, but will bring grief on John's head. The proposal needs to go to Susan, and it needs to focus on ways to *improve* productivity and retention rate in the entire Production Division at Crystar.

But *how* can John bypass Henry without creating an even worse problem with his supervisor?

The answer is simple for John: submit an Employee Suggestion. The suggestion will go directly to Susan, bypassing the shift manager, and do so appropriately. John can fill out a simple form and attach his researched proposal as the justification. John cannot criticize or complain in his proposal; he must make a positive recommendation to improve production without focusing on *why* that needs to happen.

And that is exactly what John has done in the proposal reproduced here to Susan Goforth, which was routed through her assistant division chief, Mary Marvel.

Letter of Transmittal
EMPLOYEE SUGGESTION AWARD PROGRAM
Crystar Industries
Columbia, MD 21045

DATE: July 22, 20xx
TO: Susan Goforth
THRU: Mary Marvel
FROM: John S. Jenkins, Prod B *JHJ*
SUBJ: Increased Production, Lower Attrition

The attached proposal addresses low production and high attrition in the Crystar Production Division and presents a recommended course of action to reverse both trends.

Please read the attached proposal, approve it, and take the recommended actions to implement the proposed solution.

A PROPOSAL TO INCREASE PRODUCTION AND REDUCE ATTRITION IN THE CRYSTAR PRODUCTION DIVISION

A Proposal Submitted through the Employee Suggestion Award Program to

Susan Goforth
Chief, Production Division
Crystar Enterprises

July 22, 20xx

Prepared by
John S. Jenkins
Assembly Technician
Production Branch B

EXECUTIVE SUMMARY

Crystar productions statistics for the past 24 months show that there are substantial differences in the production rates of the four branches of the Production Division—a variance of up to one-third less in one of the four branches.

In addition, attrition rates vary by up to 100 percent higher in one of the four branches.

Crystar has an effective Employee Recognition Program, yielding 144 awards for the 80 employees in three these four branches over the past 24 months. However, no employee in Branch B has been presented with any of these awards. It should come as no surprise that the branch with the highest attrition rate and the lowest production is Branch B, the one with no recognized employees.

This proposal recommends that the Employee Recognition Program be implemented in Branch B with the expectation that production will increase as a result and the attrition rate will go down in that branch.

TABLE OF CONTENTS

LIST OF ILLUSTRATIONS

INTRODUCTION

As a fast-growing producer of software applications for companies in the United States and abroad, Crystar has experienced steady growth over the past two years. The company Production Division burned, packaged, and mailed over 40,000 two-disc software programs to users over the past 24 months. This production rate is in comparison with our first five years of effort, in which we handled an aggregate of only 20,000 two-disc sets in aggregate (Crystar, Policy, iii).

As a result, two years ago, we created a four-shift Production Division with 20 packagers and one shift supervisor on each shift. These four branches have enabled Crystar to ship 24/7 for the past two years and thus keep up with our rapidly expanding customer demands. The current rate of 20,000 sets a year means that, for same-day shipping, we should be sending out 13 sets a shift, or 55 in one 24-hour period.

The production process involves seven stages:

1. Burning the two discs
2. Checking for full use (install, functionality, and file accuracy)
3. Printing disc labels that contain simplified instructions
4. Assembling the disc label jewel cases
5. Inserting disc sets in the jewel cases
6. Packaging the sets in mailers
7. Addressing labels and affixing to the packages

This process is completed by four teams in each branch and takes an average of 40 minutes from start to finish. The work is repetitive, and accuracy in each step is essential.

THE PROBLEM

Even with the introduction of four shifts, production has lagged to the extent that we now have a shipping delay of over two days, and that figure is increasing steadily each month.

The problem has occurred because three shifts consistently have met the 13 set-per-shift production rate, but Shift (Branch) B has averaged only eight sets per shift for the past 24 months (Crystar, Production, 20xx, 3; 20xy, 3), leaving a deficit in the aggregate of 3,650 fewer sets produced for that shift in the past two years.

DAILY PRODUCTION AVERAGE FOR PAST TWO YEARS				
SETS	Branch A	Branch B	Branch C	Branch D

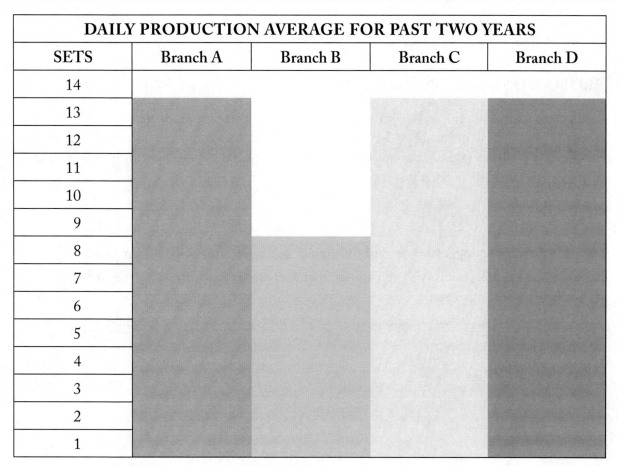

Source: Author, derived from Crystar, Production 20xx, 3; 20xy, 3.

According to the shift supervisor, the low production figures are the result of a personnel turnover rate of 20 percent every year (four employees a year) (Smith), requiring the other employees to spend part of their production time training new employees rather than in the production of the minimum number of shipments for the shift (Purcell). Each of the other three shifts has averaged a personnel turnover rate of 10 percent per year (two employees a year) (Smith).

BACKGROUND

Crystar has an active and productive Employee Recognition Program (Policy 22–25) that has resulted in an average of two awards per shift each month for the past two years for every shift but Shift B—an aggregate of 144 awards. However, Branch B has received no recognition awards at all in the past two years.

PROPOSED SOLUTION

I propose that the Employee Recognition Program be implemented for the first time in Branch B as a simple means of addressing both attrition and low production rates in that branch. The result should be that our backlog will disappear and our cost-profit ratio should increase substantially in just a few months.

RECOMMENDATION

1. The Employee Suggestion Award Program Committee approves this proposal.
2. The Committee meets with the branch manager and trains him in the use of this employee incentive tactic.
3. The Committee requires the branch to implement and sustain the program.

WORKS CITED

Crystar Industries, *Crystar Annual Report,* internal publication, *20xx.*

Crystar Industries, *Policy Manual*, internal publication, 20xx.

Crystar Industries, *Production Report for 20xx*, internal publication.

Crystar Industries, *Production Report for 20xy*, internal publication.

Purcell, Henry, Chief, Branch B, personal interview, July 13, 20xx.

Smith, Mary E., Human Relations Director, personal interview, July18, 20xx.

Summary

In this chapter, we have considered the factors involved in selecting and customizing a format for a report or proposal. The key consideration is the reader: his or her expectation—and need, and what approach is most likely to result in the desired reaction. We reviewed the planning that accompanies complex reports, including the suggestion to write the Executive Summary *first* so it can act as a guide to generating the extended version.

The inclusion of qualitative and quantitative information enhances the credibility and usefulness of any report or proposal, but the writer must be careful that the information included is unambiguous, clear, complete, and relevant.

Visual information (in the form of graphs, charts, tables, drawings, and photographs should be accurate, relevant, and integrated into the text so text and graphics can be compared together. Their inclusion significantly enhances the reader's comprehension of the material presented.

POTENTIAL ASSIGNMENTS

1. Good deed assignment:

   a. Carefully select an individual at your place of work or at some establishment with which you do business. Consider any significant act of kindness or assistance "above and beyond the call of duty" that this person has performed on your behalf or for another person. Determine the name of the individual's supervisor. Write a short note to the supervisor, describing the action that merited your appreciation. Be certain to include the *substance* of the action (its fact, quantity, and impact) in your description of the service performed, *and* request the supervisor's action to recognize his or her employee. Deliver the note to the supervisor.

   b. Then *write a memorandum to your teacher* describing the action you took *and the result*. Include a copy of your note to the supervisor as the second page of the same report that provides your teacher with your memorandum. Your note to the supervisor *must* include the supervisor's name *and* the employee's name, as well as your request for the supervisor's action. *Note:* this paper must report a *real* situation that occurred during *this* semester. This type of writing is a *basic* requirement for senior managers.

2. Write a progress report to your teacher on what you have accomplished in this class. Use headings for each section of your report. Discuss each paper you have written and what you learned from your teacher's comments. Conclude with an assessment of what you are expected to accomplish—and learn—during the remainder of the class.

3. Select a newspaper article on some topic that lends itself to the production of a graph or pie chart. Created the graph or pie chart populated with the newspaper article contents. Write a short (one-page) analytical report incorporating your graph or chart and source it in the text as (your name, derived from, article writer's last name, and page number). Include the MLA-version Works Cited entry at the end of your report.

4. Write a Point Paper to provide the information necessary for your supervisor at work or the mayor or city council where you live to act on a current issue. Include these headings (and associated discussion): Issue, Discussion, and Recommended Action, and address the point paper to the specific decision maker (include DATE, TO, FROM, and SUBJECT).

5. Create a researched (MLA-format) persuasive proposal addressed to a specific, named decision maker, stating a real problem in your workplace or community and offering a solution to the decision maker in at least 3,500 but no more than 5,000 words, including, in this order:

   A. Letter of transmittal to the decision maker

   B. Title page (containing your name, the decision maker's name as the one to whom the proposal is presented, and the title of your proposal)

C. Executive summary (covering problem, impact, proposed solution, and specific actions for decision maker to take)

D. Table of contents (each entry and page number must accurately reflect location and heading in the text)

E. List of illustrations (the illustration title and the page number where each of your illustrations appear in the text)

F. Introduction

G. A proposal organized into a series of text sections separated by specific headings and including at least two integrated graphic aids (that is, incorporated on the same pages that discuss each topic) and at least eight in-text MLA-format citations

H. Conclusion(s)

I. Recommendations: a series of step-by-step actions for the decision maker to take to implement your proposed solution

J. A Works Cited page (so titled) with at least eight references in MLA format (must follow MLA and must consist of at least three different *types* of sources—no more than three of any given type, but no more than two personal interviews). *All* references *must* be used in in-text citations in the body of the report.

Graphics *must not* be on stand-alone pages, only on the page with text that refers to them specifically. Source *all* graphics. Graphics you create would be labeled "(SOURCE: author)", and those you created from text supplied by another would be sourced as "(SOURCE: author, derived from Brown 36)" for MLA format, or "(SOURCE: author, derived from Brown 2010)" for APA format. Clip art does *not* count as one of the required graphics. Graphics should enhance the reader's understanding of the problem or solution.

At least *three* different types of sources must be used (for example, newspapers, magazines, Internet, interviews, books, or journals). No more than three of any type other than interviews may count toward the eight required and no more than two interviews may count (more of any kind of reference can be used, if necessary—they just don't count toward the eight total).

Internet sources are references found *only* on the Internet; a newspaper article obtained from the paper's website counts as a newspaper article, not as an Internet reference. Works Cited Internet sources *must* include the section title, the home page title, the author (if available), and the date of your access.

CHAPTER 5
Other Communication Issues for Managers

A. Managing and documenting meetings

B. Listening guidelines for managers

C. Managing public relations and media communication

D. Communicating in crisis

E. Change communication—internal and external

F. Intercultural communication in managing

Clarity in communications is critical—difficult to ascertain when present, extremely noticeable when absent. Most managerial writing persuades directly or informs to cause the recipient to take action. If the request is not clear, the response will not be what the manager wished to see. This chapter considers six areas of managerial communication where clarity drives the equations yielding success.

A. Managing and Documenting Meetings

Copyright © by Bob Thaves. Reprinted by permission of United Media.

The managerial writing associated with preparing for, conducting, and reporting meetings affects the roles of many participants. An obvious first question for a manager is *why* have the meeting? What is its purpose? Purpose will drive the creation of a list of required attendees and begin the creation of an agenda.

Meetings are costly: an hour involving ten mid-range or higher-level employees can cost thousands of dollars for salary investment alone. Expanding the conference electronically to involve people and elements at a distance from the physical meeting place can disrupt schedules and lead to other costs. However, as costly as a meeting might be, *not* having the meeting might prove even more costly when assumptions and miscommunication result on some critical project.

Organizing the Meeting

Meetings can waste time. A meeting in which some people dominate, there is no clear agenda, and no specific actions are assigned to specific people merely takes the attendees away from work they need to perform while producing no concrete results. Before you call a meeting, determine what needs be the outcome, who needs to be there, and what input may be required from those in attendance.

Develop an agenda *in advance* and provide it to every person who is to attend in time for that person to add the meeting to his or her schedule and prepare whatever input might be required to make the meeting a success.

Arrange for the conference room, any refreshments, notepaper, nametags, or other details, including the presence of projectors and other audiovisual equipment, teleconferencing connectivity, parking, and passes, plus other items unique to your organization or the nature of the meeting.

Come early to the meeting room, make certain all is in place, and ensure that the seating is arranged to meet your strategic requirements.

Managing the Meeting

PEANUTS reprinted by permission of Universal Uclick.

Too often the manager calls a meeting to "talk *to*" his or her subordinates. In the Peanuts cartoon, Linus is totally in charge of the agenda, the presence of his minions, and the intended outcome. A simple policy memo would suffice and not waste the attendees' time.

Begin the meeting with introductions so that everyone knows who is present and why. State the purpose and provide extra copies of the agenda for those who might have forgotten to bring theirs. Also state the expected duration.

During the meeting, listen and learn. *Every* attendee has the responsibility of moving a meeting forward—and the leader, in particular, should *listen* as well as speak, paying attention to comments *and* to nonverbal signals from those in attendance. The leader, in particular, also has the responsibility to stay in *control* of the meeting, guiding it back to the original purpose and ensuring that specific assignments are created for individuals to complete any action items that arise as a result of the meeting.

At adjournment, the leader should thank the group for attending and state when the minutes or other documentation will be available and how the documentation will be delivered (electronically or by courier or mail service, for example).

Documenting the Meeting

Time can be of the essence in distributing a *report* of a key meeting. The careful manager has the key findings written and tasks assigned *before* the meeting occurs. Then it is an easy task to alter any deviations rather than trying to build a report from whole cloth after the meeting adjourns.

Meeting documentation routinely takes on of two different approaches: *minutes of the meeting* or a *memorandum of understanding*.

If there is no serious controversy involved in the meeting discussions, a simple set of minutes will suffice. Minutes should step through the agenda items line by line, summarize discussion, and identify by name any members of the meeting with specific actions assigned. Some managers write their own minutes, but a committee may have a secretary with that responsibility. In either case, the manager reviews and approves the minutes before they are distributed. Formats for minutes can vary greatly, depending on the needs of the organization, but generally they take the form of a simple memorandum with the required TO, FROM, SUBJECT, and DATE elements, plus the body in paragraph or bullet format, with or without headings to separate specific topics.

The topic and content of some meetings might be confidential. See Chapter 6 for some precautions that the manager must take to safeguard the privacy of individuals while preserving the confidentiality of proceedings. Content, distribution, and handling of such minutes while in route and after delivery are critical elements of confidentiality.

The Memorandum of Understanding is more formal, addresses mission-critical decisions, and is signed by the principals as a confirmation of their agreement to abide by the decisions reached at the meeting. The format for this type of document also varies according to the dictates of the two organizations involved, but generally this document will be a letter with the to organizations' seals or logos and the title "Memorandum of Understanding." The letter will be dated and will contain the signature blocks for both principals at the end of the specific content. Usually, the content will be separated into key sections, each introduced by a heading.

B. Listening Guidelines for Managers

"We have two ears and one tongue so that we would listen more and talk less."

—Diogenes of Sinope, Greek philosopher (c. 404–323 B.C.)

There is a distinct difference between *hearing* (a passive effort) words and *listening* (an active effort) to messages. Listening takes extra effort, but makes all the difference in determining whether or not communication has occurred and how effective it has been. We usually have no trouble listening if (1) we need information, (2) we need to understand something the speaker is trying to say, (3) we want to learn something, or (4) the speaker is entertaining. The problems come from not *wanting* to listen. Barriers to listening include (1) assumptions, (2) focus on what the hearer wants to say instead of what the speaker *is* saying, (3) preoccupation with some other issue, (4) a perception that the messenger is without value and thus the message will be of no value as well. Not hearing is *always* controlled by mind of the listener, and it is a condition driven by the listener's attitude.

Assumptions

The movie *The Flight of the Phoenix* (1965, *staring James Stewart* http://www.imdb.com/title/tt0059183/) explores the damage that assumptions can cause. A cargo plane goes down in a sandstorm in the Sahara with less than a dozen men on board. One of the passengers is an airplane designer, who comes up with the idea of taking off the undamaged wing and using it as the basis for an airplane they will build to escape before their food and water run out. In the midst of this desperate struggle for survival, the group discovers that the designer makes *model* airplanes and they thus they lose all cohesion. Although he asserts that the principles are the same, the designer's demeanor adds to the assumptions of the rest of the group that he is not credible. The movie explores the way each member of the group comes to believe in the designer's abilities and help restore both his credibility and the group purpose before time runs out and they die in the desert.

If you don't hear because you are focusing on what *you* want to say, you are worried about something else, or you have "tuned out" the speaker because of his or her personality or your perception that he or she has nothing worthwhile to say, then try these five strategies recommended by Bell and Smith (From *Management Communication, Third Edition* by Arthur H. Bell and Dayle M. Smith. Copyright © 2010 by John Wiley & Sons, Inc. Reproduced with permission of John Wiley & Sons, Inc.) to listen effectively:

1. Focus on facts and issues, not on personalities.

2. Show by your facial expressions and your willingness to listen that you want to understand the other person's position and feelings.

3. Dignify and clarify the other person's position by repeating in your own words what you understand the person to be saying.

4. Present alternatives in the form of possible options, not direct objections to the person's position.

5. Directly ask for the person's input on how to resolve matters of disagreement or impasse.

C. Managing Public Relations and Media Communication

"The greatest problem with communication is the illusion that it exists."

—George Bernard Shaw

"The jury will disregard the witness's last remarks."

From *The New Yorker, October 3, 1977* by Lee Lorenz. Copyright © 1977 by Lee Lorenz. Reprinted by permission.

The Lorenz cartoon illustrates a profound truth: once a manager speaks, he cannot *un*-speak.

Public and media communication presents the organization, *not* the individual. The manager must realize at all times that he or she is speaking for an entity, not for him- or herself. Effective media relations are critical to an organization's survival. Whether the organization is service-oriented or product-focused, public opinion can either stimulate support for or discourage support for the product or service involved. How a recall is handled, for example, can either destroy a company or build support. Normally, an organization will designate a spokesperson in advance, usually the Public Affairs Director, and *all* personnel will be instructed to refer all public and media inquiries to that individual—thus reducing the number of opportunities for misstatements by individuals who do not have the information available to speak with accuracy.

All the public ever knows about an organization comes either from personal experience or from media (paid or unsolicited).

Most Public Affairs Directors have three resources prepared for communicating with the public:

1. A list of key contacts and multiple ways of getting in touch of each

2. A series of prepared statements on all aspects of the organization

3. A crisis action plan

D. Communicating in Crisis

Crisis management has a number of equally important ingredients:

1. Preplanning. By anticipating the major types of crises that require interaction with the public, the organization can avoid confusion, misstatements, and deadly delays in dealing with the issues.

2. Established communication channels. When *everyone* in the organization knows who the crisis team is and how information is to be provided to them, there will be fewer delays in providing decision makers with the facts they need to abate the crisis. Further, if the spokesperson is designated in advance, senior management will be able to avoid speaking "candidly" and off the cuff—practices that dig the hole much, much deeper.

3. Dealing with the facts candidly. Cover-up and denial techniques might seem instinctively appropriate, but they *never* work. It's far better to admit error and move forward with the solution. This tactic leaves the media with nothing to feed on.

4. Creating and *using* a crisis management team well before any crisis exists. The team will explore all the reasonable "what ifs" and actively *plan* to manage foreseeable crises for the organization.

Preparing the Communication

Most often, the initial communication from an organization comes in the form of press releases either handed to or read to the media. Crises are so prevalent in our society that there are entire websites now are devoted to crisis management planning, templates for action, communication, and follow-up. A practical formula for the initial press release is:

1. **Identification of spokesperson and contact information:** "I am John/Jane Doe, Director of Public Affairs for the Hot Spot Fireworks Company. I will be your contact during this crisis."

2. ***Short* statement of the crisis:** "At 5:43 this morning, an explosion destroyed our plant in Podunk, Wyoming. This event left five of our employees dead and two missing. To our knowledge, there has been no injury to others or damage to property other than our plant."

3. **What caused the problem and what we are doing about it:** "You can appreciate the fact that details are still sketchy as to the cause of the explosion. Within 15 minutes after the blast, we sent a team to the site to help search for the missing employees and investigate the cause of this disaster. Our CEO is meeting with the families of those employees killed in the blast and will help them address their emotional and financial needs during this trying time. We expect reports from the team every two hours, beginning at 10:00 this morning, and will keep the media apprised as we begin to understand what happened. As a precaution, we have shut down the operation of our other facility, in Last Chance, Wyoming, and have dispatched a second team to that site. The two teams are in constant communication and we hope to have a quick resolution to this situation. Thank you."

Notice the absence of any statement about the company maintaining the highest standards of safety, this being the first incident in 15 years, and the like. Statements such as these leave the organization wide open to a feeding frenzy from the media and make what is at best a terrible tragedy for the employees who died and their families have suffered irreplaceable loss into a bubbling cauldron of fear: "The second plant is only a half-mile from my home; we are all going to die!" Questions like "Just how safe is your production process?" and "Is it true you can't keep employees more than six months because of the inherent danger?" won't be encouraged by the statement developed by management *in advance* of this type of crisis.

Dan Ammerman observed:

> What the media does not understand, they view negatively. That which they view negatively, they express with outrage. You have to make sure they understand. It is your responsibility to be understood, not their responsibility to understand. If you expect the media to get a quick Master's Degree in your business in order to understand what you are saying, you have already failed. In a crisis we want you to know what you are saying and we want the media to understand....

> Some of us have a language picked up in our field over a lifetime that most people do not understand ... technical words and phrases. The military speaks in acronyms. Some corporations do as well. Speak to the tenth grade level of understanding. Eliminate technical jargon whenever possible. If you must use it, explain what it means.

> The easiest way to get into quicksand is to respond with personal opinions. No one can fault a person who responds when asked for a personal opinion on something about which everyone is talking. However, you must remember

that you are the company. You cannot publicly separate yourself from the company image. You are being interviewed mainly because of who you are in a company context, not who you are privately. When you offer a personal opinion that differs from the company's opinion, you appear to contradict yourself, creating a negative perception which is difficult to overcome....

For example, Police Chief Daryl Gates of the Los Angeles Police Department responded to a media barrage because a police suspect was killed while being subdued with a choke hold. The inquiry should have centered on the question of excessive force. Chief Gates, in his attempt to explain why a choke hold would kill a black suspect easier than a white one, said that blacks are built differently than normal people. That unfortunate comment became the story that spread nationally. The media lost interest in the original story. (Ammerman 1994, © Dan Ammerman. Reprinted by permission.)

E. Change Communication—Internal and External

The creation of policy memoranda, announcements of change in mission or personnel numbers, and the innate fallout that such communication brings, is of critical importance to the manager.

A first consideration for the writer of policy or change communication is what the effect will be on the reader—the effect *and* the reaction. Change is *never* easy to accept, even in the worst of times, for fear that what happens next will be worse yet. Niccolo Machiavelli (a strategic advisor to royal leaders) wrote in *The Prince* In 1513:

> There is nothing more difficult to carry out, nor more doubtful of success, nor more dangerous to handle, than to initiate a new order of things.

> For the reformer has enemies in all who profit by the old order, and only lukewarm defenders in all those who would profit by the new order;

> This lukewarmness arises partly from fear of their adversaries, who have the law in their favor; and partly from the incredulity of mankind, who do not truly believe in anything new until they have had actual experience of it. (Machiavelli 1513, p. 51)

The Stages of Change Management

1. Keeping Secrets

The management of change is quite difficult because it involves the strategy used by the traditional professional riverboat gamblers of a century and a half ago. The gambler's "poker face" did not give away the value of the cards he was holding until it was too late for his opponent to react.

When the management decision to expand or downsize, reorganize, or merge is under study, the process must be kept secret from the workforce, from the competition, and from the public for the same reason—to prevent any opponents from forming a counterstrategy that would defeat the developing management plan. A prematurely leaked exposure of the "what if" stage of such planning sends one message—and one message only: "we are in for a *big* change!" When employees get wind of a "big change," they circle the wagons or abandon ship. Either way, there is a major disruption in production and morale. Consequently, the first stage of change communication is a strict need-to-know basis and keeping all written documentation to a minimum. The survival of the organizational change contemplated, *and*, often, those who propose the change, is dependent on the initial confidentiality of the process. Truly, the secrets to the plan's survival are timing, confidentiality, and staging the release of information.

Those who write as, to, or for managers in such a situation have to be accurate, circumspect, and discreet. You should write every sentence as though it will later be used as evidence in a court of law—because that has indeed happened before with such communication.

Your planning must take into consideration the reaction of every possible player, from the workforce to the customers and to other departments and businesses. You really cannot afford to make a single announcement and relax because "the cat is out of the bag" without contemplating *in advance* what the reaction will be and planning for that reaction—those people who have suffered pain by your organizational change will become even more upset to the extent that they may cause significant negative reaction to what has just happened if you have not addressed their concerns in advance.

2. Going Public

Correspondence created to explain the change must always be positive and upbeat. Such communication must also be final in nature, announcing a deed that has been done, not a tentative "we're gonna' try this for a while." Special care must be taken to handle obvious concerns in the announcement, and the normal format for such an announcement would include headings with separate sections to announce the change, provide implementation steps, address—and resolve—concerns, and provide contact information *and the availability of a contact person/group* to take care of concerns that emerge after the initial announcement has been absorbed.

This communication scenario is quite like crisis communication, and the strategies employed to prevent corporate disaster are the same.

In *Beyond the Wall of Resistance* (Austin, TX: Bard Press, 2010, 12–14), Rick Maurer notes four reasons why 70 percent of all managerial changes fail. The manager:

1.   Assumes that understanding equals support and commitment
2.   Underestimates the potential power of employee and management engagement

3.   Fails to appreciate the power of fear, and/or

4.   Fails to acknowledge how even a slight lack of trust and confidence in leaders can kill an otherwise good idea.

Maurer notes that success comes when the manager has followed this pattern, which he calls "The Cycle of Change" (2010, 18) and which he notes was adapted from the "Cycle of Experience" developed by the Gestalt Institute of Chicago. He says that managers will institute successful change when they:

1.   Make a compelling case for change

2.   Get started on the right foot

3.   Keep the change alive (testing, monitoring, making certain that the system works)

4.   Get back on track to stay on schedule, within budget, and meet original goals

5.   Recognize the time to move on and do so

Maurer's book details a series of strategies to employ—or to avoid—in addressing each one of these steps in the process.

Change management principles have changed little in the 500 years since Machiavelli described them in *The Prince*, but they are of critical importance if the writing for, as, or to managers regarding change in the work place is to be effective.

F. Intercultural Communication in Managing

Americans use eye contact to indicate rapt attention; some cultures demonstrate their attentiveness by averting their eyes. Conversational distance varies from culture to culture; some negotiate at six inches, others at six feet. Some get right to the point (the "bottom line"); others are insulted if observations about the day, your health, and the condition of your family are not explored first. Body language, including gestures, is significantly cultural in nature. What is expected in one area of the world might be highly offensive in another.

Queen Cleopatra of Egypt exemplified masterful ability in the realm of multicultural management. Stacy Schiff (*Cleopatra, A Life*, New York: Little, Brown and Company, 2010) notes that Cleopatra (69–30 BC) was the last Ptolemy of Macedonian descent. Her name means "Glory of the Fatherland" in Greek, which she spoke fluently. She also spoke fluent Latin (bearing children to both Julius Caesar and, later, to her husband Marc Antony) and the language of Egypt. She spoke the languages of the Syrians, the Medians, and the Thracians, Hebrew, and Troglodyte (Ethiopian)—altogether nine languages—and was the first Ptolemy to learn Egyptian, the language of the seven million people she ruled (Schiff 2010, 24–33). Because of her ability to communicate effectively in nine languages, her era on the Egyptian throne was exceptionally successful. She knew not only the language of her neighbors, but also their cultures and their focus. As a consequence, her treaties were honored, her decisions were fair and tolerated by all, she was the first Ptolemy actually liked and supported by the Egyptians, and she kept the threat of Roman conquest at bay for 22 years.

So, if you want your multicultural communication to be effective, pay attention not only to language differences, but cultural practices as well, and create correspondence that lays out issues and recommendations clearly, without offense.

Be careful! When you write in a multicultural environment, be certain that you truly understand the culture you are communicating with and are not merely assuming that a stereotype reflects reality.

Summary

Clarity in communications is critical—difficult to ascertain when present and extremely noticeable when absent. Most managerial writing informs to cause the recipient to take action. If the request is not clear, the response will not be what the manager wished to see. This chapter considered six areas of managerial communication in which clarity drives the equations yielding success: managing and documenting meetings, listening guidelines for managers, managing public relations and media communication, communicating in crisis, change communication (internal and external), and intercultural communication in managing.

Meetings work only when they have a good purpose, everyone knows about them in time to prepare and come, they stick to a predetermined agenda, and action items are assigned clearly.

Managers who fail to listen are not communicating, and the results are never pleasant. Listening takes effort, and effort requires focus. Failure to listen rests with the listener and is always a matter of attitude.

Public and media communication presents the organization, *not* the individual. Everything a consumer knows about an organization comes from the media or from personal contact. The effective spokesperson for an organization (usually the Public Affairs Director) commonly maintains three tools for successful media relations: a list of key contacts and multiple ways of getting in touch of each, a series of prepared statements on all aspects of the organization, and a crisis action plan.

The crisis action plan helps the organization spokesperson deal effectively with the public and the media in times of crisis. Crises *will* come, so preparation is essential. There should be one spokesperson, everyone should know and follow the crisis action plan, and there should be some prepared statements to assist in reassuring the public and satisfying the media that the organization is on top of the issue.

Change communication has two phases: confidentiality and public announcement. Premature release of a plan will cause morale and retention problems for the organization or the public; announcing change without addressing obvious issues the change generates will have the same effect, because introducing change is never popular.

Intercultural communication requires the communicator to be sensitive to cultural and regional differences because they can produce barriers that block the results the communicator desires.

SUGGESTED ASSIGNMENTS

1. **Internal reorganization (change).** As the Division chief you have met with senior leadership and the extensive deliberation that resulted has led to the need for you to announce the reorganization of your division. Effective in three days, you will have three departments instead of four. The duties of the Accounting Department functions will be split between the Procurement Department and the Sales Department. The eight employees in Accounting will be assigned (four each) to the other two departments and the former chief of Accounting will be promoted and thus transferred to the Staff Advisory Council in another location by senior management.

2. **Managing meetings.** Write a one-page memo to your workforce announcing a meeting to discuss the reorganization of your office. Include a one-page agenda assigning responsibility for at least two reports by specific members of your team to be presented at the meeting.

3. **Crisis management.** Harry Plume, the outgoing chief of the Accounting Department, is quite popular with his eight employees. At the staff meeting (see Assignment 2), there will likely be a nasty scene when they discover that they are being split up as a team and losing their popular leader. Write an Action Plan to address this issue, including a prepared statement to be memorized and presented at the meeting.

4. **Meeting minutes.** Draft the minutes of the meeting discussed in Assignment 2, including the outcome of the anticipated crisis (Assignment 3) to be sent to all participants *and* to William Buxley, CEO.

5. **Intercultural communication.** Write a letter for your CEO, William Buxley, to send to Ms. Ankh-set-seg Kaahn, Chairwoman of the Board for the State Department Store (the "ikh delguur" or "big shop") in Ulaanbaator, Mongolia, to invite trade negotiations for the purchase of cashmere sweaters from her store for resale by your business in the United States. Your company is Sweater-Mart, 1415 Stretchnwear Drive, Dunkirk, Maryland 20736.

CHAPTER 6

Planning and Policy Communication

A. Strategic planning

B. Writing mission and vision statements

C. Writing the business plan

D. Communicating policy

E. Ethics and law for managers

How forcible are right words.
—Bible, KJV, Job 6:25

Planning and policy communication tasks engage only managers and the people who write to or for them. Unlike the daily communication tasks of business writing, the focus of planning and policy activities is to change lives. Mission and vision statements capture the focus of the organization now and in the foreseeable future, as do business plans (which should include both a mission statement and the company vision). In this chapter, we will review all of these critical areas, plus consider the impact of ethical decisions and the relationship of the manager to legislation designed to protect customers, the workforce, and the organization.

Businesses, corporations, government agencies, and other organizations drawn together for a common purpose exist in the present and in the future simultaneously. The daily communication required to keep such entities running smoothly focus on present requirements. Planning for the future and shaping policy to carry the company toward that future are tasks to which managers devote considerable effort.

A *Far Side* cartoon of several decades ago has one polar bear lifting the front of an igloo as another watches an Eskimo running away. The first bear is saying sarcastically, "I lift, you grab, was that a little too hard for you, Carl?" The plan was simple: one bear opens the lunch box, the other extracts the meal. But two unexpected things happened on execution: (1) the lunch chose not to cooperate, and (2) the plan left no time to practice eye-paw coordination. The result was the typical outcome of insufficient planning when executed.

Like most managerial scenarios, the opportunity for a repeat performance is practically nonexistent.

A. Strategic Planning

Carter McNamara of Authenticity Consulting notes:

> Simply put, *strategic planning determines where an organization is going over the next year or more, how it's going to get there and how it'll know if it got there or not.* The focus of a strategic plan is usually on the entire organization, while the focus of a business plan is usually on a particular product, service, or program.
>
> There are a variety of perspectives, models, and approaches used in strategic planning. The way that a strategic plan is developed depends on the nature of the organization's leadership, culture of the organization, complexity of the organization's environment, size of the organization, expertise of planners, etc. For example, there are a variety of strategic planning models, including goals-based, issues-based, organic, and scenario (some would assert that scenario planning is more of a technique than model).
>
> 1. Goals-based planning is probably the most common and starts with focus on the organization's mission (and vision and/or values), goals to work toward the mission, strategies to achieve the goals, and action planning (who will do what and by when).
>
> 2. Issues-based strategic planning often starts by examining issues facing the organization, strategies to address those issues and action plans.
>
> 3. Organic strategic planning might start by articulating the organization's vision and values, and then action plans to achieve the vision while adhering to those values. Some planners prefer a particular approach to planning, e.g., appreciative inquiry. (From http://managementhelp.org/ plan_dec/str_plan/str_plan.htm by Carter McNamara. Reprinted by permission.)

Philip Blackerby, in "History of Strategic Planning," notes that the concept of strategic planning was introduced by the ancient Greeks. He reports that "In the early 1920s, Harvard Business School developed the Harvard Policy Model, one of the first strategic planning methodologies for private businesses" (http://www.blackerbyassoc.com/history.html). In the 1950s, Secretary of Defense Robert S. McNamara introduced the concept for defense management, and the Government Performance and Results Act of 1993 (GPRA, P.L. 103-62) requires all federal agencies to write a strategic plan that includes a mission statement; outcome-based goals and objectives; descriptions of how goals will be achieved, resource needs, and how objectives will link to performance plans; a list of external influences on goals; and a program evaluation schedule. The GPRA also requires agencies to write an annual performance plan and to submit an annual performance report comparing actual to planned performance levels. For complying agencies, the GPRA provides for waivers of administrative procedural requirements over staffing levels, salaries, and funding transfers. The bill established pilot programs for early testing of these ideas, including a pilot test of "performance budgeting," which relates levels of planned outcomes to corresponding budget levels.

For those who write strategic plans, there is an entire body of literature on the subject. Moreover, the concepts associated with this managerial tool have developed over the course of half a century. As a consequence, there are multiple ways to use the concepts and diverse ways of labeling the steps. For this course, it is sufficient that you become familiar with the basic concepts, terms, and desired outcomes of the process.

Terminology

A *strategic goal* is a long-term desired outcome. To achieve this outcome, planners will develop and implement short-range *tactical goals*. Tactical goals are the steps required to reach the ultimate, strategic goal. Inevitably, barriers will crop up, making achievement of these intermediate steps (the tactical goals) difficult or impossible, thus side-tracking the organization's realization of its strategic goal. These barriers come in the form of *issues* and *concerns*. These barriers differ in intensity and difficulty to overcome. Issues are "show-stoppers." Until they are dealt with, the tactical goal will not be met and progress toward achieving the strategic goal will come to a halt. Concerns are worrisome, but usually easier to address. Basically, they are the *fears* that things may go wrong.

To combat either an *issue* or a *concern*, the planner employs a *strategy* or specific approach to dealing with the barrier. To implement the strategy, the planner engages *tactics*. Tactics are those intermediate steps that result in the strategy being effective. Those six terms constitute the core language of strategic planning. A planner sets *tactical goals* to achieve a long-term *strategic goal* and addresses *issues* and *concerns* blocking progress toward achieving a tactical goal with specific *strategies* he or she implements via *tactics*.

The concept is exceptionally flexible. For example, your *strategic goal* might be to get an undergraduate degree. To do so, you have to pass this course (among others), so one *tactical goal* is to obtain a good grade on this course. You might have some *concerns* about doing so; however, doing the work on time and as directed is a good *strategy* to avoid complications in achieving your tactical goal. Your *tactics* in implementing your strategy will include keeping up with assignments, following instructions, and clarifying directions that you don't understand through discussing your questions with your teacher. Likewise, an *issue* might be fear of obtaining a bad grade on a key assignment. Your *strategy* might be to analyze *exactly* what the teacher is looking for and focus on each requirement. If your worst fears materialize and you do get the bad grade, then your strategy to minimize its effect might be to discuss the grade with your teacher and the *tactics* might be to seek an opportunity to redo the assignment or turn in extra-credit work.

Flexibility means that you can apply the same process to obtaining your master's degree. Now, obtaining an undergraduate degree has become a *tactical* goal, and so on.

The value of strategic planning is that the process focuses on results and the results focus on the organization (or individual) mission and goals. The terminology guides planners as they strive to accomplish a common set of objectives. Managerial writers who use the terminology correctly will communicate effectively with upper-level managers and all affected by this type of planning.

B. Writing Mission and Vision Statements

A *mission statement* tells what the organization is doing right now; a *vision statement* tells what the organization *should* be doing to survive in the future. The combination of mission and vision statements creates the basis for stating the *strategic goal(s)* necessary for the organization to attain the vision of the future.

The 1993 *mission* of the University of Maryland University College (UMUC) was "To extend the educational resources of the University System throughout the State and around the world" (*UMUC Faculty Guide*).

In 2011, the written description of the UMUC mission was fundamentally changed:

> The mission of University of Maryland University College is to offer top-quality educational opportunities to adult students in Maryland, the nation, and the world, setting the global standard of excellence in adult education. By offering academic programs that are respected, accessible, and affordable, UMUC broadens the range of career opportunities available to students, improves their lives, and maximizes their economic and intellectual contributions to Maryland and the nation. (http://www.umuc.edu/gen/mission.shtml, by University of Maryland University College. © by University of Maryland University College. Reprinted by permission.)

In addition, the university added seven core values (focused only on what the university should do for students, but not addressing expectations of what the students should do for the institution):

STUDENTS FIRST

These are the people who make our work possible.

ACCOUNTABILITY

We are each responsible for our overall success.

DIVERSITY

Each individual brings value to our efforts and results.

INTEGRITY

Our principles and standards are never compromised.

EXCELLENCE

Outstanding quality is the hallmark of our work.

INNOVATION

We advance so others can benefit from our leadership.

RESPECT

The rights and feelings of others are always considered.

http://www.umuc.edu/gen/about.shtml, by University of Maryland University College. © by University of Maryland University College. Reprinted by permission.

The mission statement should address what the organization is in business to do, who it should do that service or develop that product for, and how it will accomplish that mission. Note that the 1993 mission statement ("To extend the educational resources of the University System throughout the State and around the world") is missing some key ingredients.

Vision statements are the other bookend. UMUC does not offer a vision statement directly on their website; however, this language suggests what it might be:

A World Class University Designed for You

Founded in 1947, University of Maryland University College (UMUC) is one of 11 accredited, degree-granting institutions in the University of Maryland (USM). Offering a broad range of cutting-edge classes, UMUC has earned a worldwide reputation for excellence as a comprehensive virtual university and for focusing on the unique educational and professional development needs of adult students.

The school's variety of learning formats afford maximum convenience to busy adult students who must balance the demands of full-time jobs, family, and community responsibilities.

Working adults, military personnel, and other students around the globe are achieving their academic goals through UMUC's innovative educational options, including online instruction, accelerated academic programs, and classroom-based courses taught during the daytime, evenings, and week-ends. (http://www.umuc.edu/gen/about.shtml, by University of Maryland University College. © by University of Maryland University College. Reprinted by permission.)

And page 4 of the current UMUC Strategic Plan, which is accessible on the website, does include that statement:

UMUC will be the leading global university distinguished by the quality of our education, commitment to our students' success, and accessibility to our programs. (http://www.umuc.edu/gen/strategic_plan.pdf by University of Maryland University College. © by University of Maryland University College. Reprinted by permission.)

Components of an Effective Mission Statement

McMurry University, a Methodist university in Abilene, Texas, offers this description of the components of an effective mission statement:

> Mission statements can and do vary in length, content, format and specific- ity. Most practitioners and academicians of strategic management consider an effectively written mission statement to exhibit nine characteristics or mission statement components. Since a mission statement is often the most visible and public part of the strategic management process, it is important that it include most, if not all, of these essential components. Components and corresponding questions that a mission statement should answer are given here.
>
> 1.   Customers: Who are the enterprise's customers?
> 2.   Products or services: What are the firm's major products or services?
> 3.   Markets: Where does the firm compete?
> 4.   Technology: What is the firm's basic technology?
> 5.   Concern for survival, growth, and profitability: What is the firm's commitment towards economic objectives?
> 6.   Philosophy: What are the basic beliefs, core values, aspirations and philosophical priorities of the firm?
> 7.   Self-concept: What are the firm's major strengths and competitive advantages?
> 8.   Concern for public image: What is the firm's public image?
> 9.   Concern for employees: What is the firm's attitude/orientation towards employees?

This is the mission of McMurry University:

> The mission of McMurry University is to provide a Christian liberal arts and professional education that prepares students for a fulfilling life of leadership and service. (http://www.mcm.edu/newsite/web/aboutmcm/who_we_are.htm. © by McMurray University. Reprinted by permission.)

How many of the nine possible components does this mission statement address? What is missing? Does that make a difference, or is this a "good" mission statement?

C. Writing the Business Plan

A *business plan* is a formal document that lays out what the purpose of your organization is (your mission statement), how it is structured, how it operates, your financial assets and how your organization will meet its financial obligations, the résumés of key employees, and your business model. The plan can serve numerous functions simultaneously:

1. It helps senior management get organized and focus on priorities.

2. It helps employees understand the function and values of the organization.

3. It attracts funds from lenders and investors.

4. It sells the company to perspective purchasers.

5. It helps customers understand and support the organization.

The plan needs to be clear, accurate, comprehensive, effectively structured, and tailored to each audience it is to reach. It needs to *reach* each audience, as well, or it—and the organization—may fail.

Business Plan Structure

The typical plan has these components:

Cover page: Organization name, address, phone number, name of chief executive.

Table of Contents

Executive Summary

The Organization: Basic information about the organization (past, present, future; structure, succession, stock/share plan, management team, guiding principles).

Mission Statement

Vision Statement

The Market: Your assessment of targeted customer groups, potential ones, and success of efforts to date [include testimonials].

The Product/Service: Components, what makes it special, warranties, what is *not* provided.

Sales and Promotion: Carrying out your marketing plan, internal assets, public relations.

Finances: Past, present, and future. Include cash flow projections, profit-and-loss statements, balance sheets.

Personnel: Résumés for each employee with a focus on their experience and what they contribute to the organization.

Because the business plan is written in sections, it is possible to create the plan in any given order and it is also possible for different teams or organizations to craft different segments of the plan. If so, a single editor needs to review the completed project, put every component into the appropriate sequences, and determine that the tone and approach stay constant throughout the entire plan.

D. Communicating Policy

Dean Harrison Edwards at Midwestern University thought he had a happy faculty. The three or four cronies he ate with regularly seemed supportive of his efforts. In fact, the faculty was on the verge of mutiny over a number of issues, including delayed salary increases, class cancellations, and tenure denials. Faculty "filters," therefore, were especially active as professors read the following memo from Dean Edwards:

> In my position as Dean of this university, it gives me deep pleasure to announce the Visiting Scholars Lecture Series. Four established and respected experts will present lecture/discussion sessions in the fields of computer science, literature, history, and art. Representatives from our faculty will serve as university hosts for these scholars.

The Dean was dumbfounded to learn that his faculty had decided to boycott the lecture series, calling his memo "insulting."

What aroused the faculty?

Filters to pick out of this memo for emphasis:
1. "In my position as Dean … it gives me deep pleasure": He's patting himself on the back again. Who cares what gives him pleasure?
2. "established and respected experts" He's as much as saying that none of us are established and respected!
3. "in the fields of computer science, literature, history, and art": How expected that the Dean should choose the fields of his cronies!
4. "faculty representatives will serve": Notice that he doesn't ask us—he tells us what we'll do. The guests are called "scholars" while we're just "representatives"!

If we wish to place blame for this communication disaster, the faculty certainly could be more charitable in its interpretation of the memo. However, the primary responsibility probably falls upon the dean as a leader who failed to consider the presence and activity of powerful filters that distorted the message he meant to send.

The point: it is not enough to mean well in sending a message. We must design messages well to counter the effects of powerful and often subconscious filters active in our readers and hearers." (From *Management Communication, Third Edition* by Arthur H. Bell and Dayle M. Smith. © 2010 by John Wiley & Sons, Inc. Reproduced with permission of John Wiley & Sons, Inc.)

Consequently, policy documents, because they introduce change, are actually rather difficult to write well. The basic message—there is going to be a change in the way we conduct business with an explanation of *what* and *when*—usually is quite straightforward. However, because *any* change generates emotional reactions *and* raises questions, and because unanswered questions cause a magnification of emotional reactions—the wording introducing the change is crucial. Hence the managerial writer who creates such a piece of communication must be exceptionally careful in what is said, how it is said, and what is not said in the announcement.

E. Ethics and Law for Managers

If you have integrity, nothing else matters. If you don't have integrity, nothing else matters.

—Senator Alan K. Simpson

(http://thinkexist.com/quotation/if_you_have_integrity-nothing_else_matters-if_you/ 343397.html)

The Institute of Business Ethics published a study in April 2006 by Simon Webley and Elise More ("Does Business Ethics Pay?") that concluded: "companies with codes of ethics ... out-perform in financial and other indicators those companies who say they do not have a code" (http://www.darden.virginia.edu/corporate-ethics/news/bp060427.htm). Basically, a code of ethics is a best practice for all businesses—and those who write to, for, or as managers must be aware of the ethical standards their company follows and incorporate those standards in their writing. If the company has not adopted a code of ethics, then it is an obvious conclusion that the writer should adhere to such principles as an individual.

Copyright © Boeing. Reprinted by permission.

The Boeing Code of Conduct outlines expected behaviors for all Boeing employees.

> Boeing will conduct its business fairly, impartially, in an ethical and proper manner, and in full compliance with all applicable laws and regulations. In conducting its business, integrity must underlie all company relationships, including those with customers, suppliers, communities and among employees. The highest standards of ethical business conduct are required of Boeing employees in the performance of their company responsibilities. Employees will not engage in conduct or activity that may raise questions as to the company's honesty, impartiality, reputation or otherwise cause embarrassment to the company.

> Employees will ensure that:

> • They do not engage in any activity that might create a conflict of interest for the company or for themselves individually.

- They do not take advantage of their Boeing position to seek personal gain through the inappropriate use of Boeing or non-public information or abuse of their position. This includes not engaging in insider trading.

- They will follow all restrictions on use and disclosure of information. This includes following all requirements for protecting Boeing information and ensuring that non-Boeing proprietary information is used and disclosed only as authorized by the owner of the information or as otherwise permitted by law.

- They observe that fair dealing is the foundation for all of our transactions and interactions.

- They will protect all company, customer and supplier assets and use them only for appropriate company approved activities.

- Without exception, they will comply with all applicable laws, rules and regulations.

- They will promptly report any illegal or unethical conduct to management or other appropriate authorities (i.e., Ethics, Law, Security, EEO).

Every employee has the responsibility to ask questions, seek guidance and report suspected violations of this Code of Conduct. Retaliation against employees who come forward to raise genuine concerns will not be tolerated. (http://www.boeing.com/companyoffices/aboutus/ethics/code_of_conduct.pdf)

Moral and Legal Issues

Suppose you have a problem employee, one who is not responding to counseling, so you keep a detailed file on when you have talked to him or her and what was said. Finally, the relationship has deteriorated to the point that you must give him or her a termination notice. What will happen when you give the employee the notice and show him or her the file? Do you know your rights? Do you know the employee's rights? Before you start taking notes, have a long and earnest discussion with your general counsel or your Human Resources Department. Noting *facts* is one thing; inserting personal opinion quite another.

Here are a few concepts and regulations you should know:

Invasion of Privacy

The American jurisprudence system has been explained as, "My right to swing my fist ends where the other man's nose begins" (variously attributed to Oliver Wendell Holmes, Jr.— http://ffrf.org/day/view/03/08/, for example, and Zecheraih Chafee, Jr—recorded in "Freedom of Speech in Wartime", 32 Harvard Law Review 932, 957 (1919)). (*The Autocrat at the Breakfast Table*).

Basically, everyone has rights, and there are rules to govern how those rights must be protected. Your employees do not give up their right to privacy completely when they come to work for your company. You (and they) need to be clear about what constitutes fair access and what does not.

The Federal Government has been guilty of invasion of privacy—the McCarthy era comes to mind, as do various FBI "lists." An attempt to correct this violation of personal rights was made by establishing the Freedom of Information Act in 1966 (5 U.S.C. § 552, As Amended By Public Law No. 104-231, 110 Stat. 3048—to see the entire Act, visit http://www.justice.gov/oip/foia_updates/Vol_XVII_4/page2.htm).

The Rehabilitation Act of 1973 (19 U.S.C.A. §§ 791, 793, 794) prohibits disability discrimination. AN ACT

> To replace the Vocational REHABILITATION ACT, to extend and revise the authorization of grants to States for vocational REHABILITATION services, with special emphasis on services to those with the most severe handicaps, to expand special Federal responsibilities and research and training programs with respect to handicapped individuals, to establish special responsibilities in the Secretary of Health, Education, and Welfare for coordination of all programs with respect to handicapped individuals within the Department of Health, Education, and Welfare, and for other purposes.

Americans with Disabilities Act (ADA) (42 U.S.C.A. §§ 12101–12213), Employment Discrimination and the ADA Titles I and II of the ADA prohibit discrimination because of disability. The Equal Employment Opportunity Commission (EEOC) is the federal agency that oversees the employment-discrimination provisions of the ADA (http://www.eeoc.gov).

Summary

True managerial writing differs from routine business communication in that it is designed to change lives. The content of such writing addresses strategic planning, mission and vision statements, business plans, communicating policy, and understanding and incorporating ethics and legal ramifications in organizational communications.

POTENTIAL ASSIGNMENTS

1. David Jones is your office manager at Widgets Я Us. He has insisted that *all* employees must work one specific shift, even though that presents serious child care issues for some employees and customer access cannot occur before the office opens at 9:00 a.m. or after it closes at 4:00 p.m. You would like to see the office stagger shifts to cover a ten-hour 8:00 a.m. to 6:00 p.m. workday, but when you approached David, he dismissed the idea as "ridiculous." Develop a Strategic Plan that will describe the steps you will pursue to present this proposal to the owner, Mary Evans. Include all six terms used in this concept (strategic goal, tactical goal, issue, concern, strategy, tactic). You can bypass David with this proposal by presenting it as an Employee Suggestion Program entry. Such documents go directly from the employee to Mary Evans.

2. Develop a mission statement for Widgets Я Us.

3. Write a business plan for Widgets Я Us. Include sections for employee résumés and financial matters, but do not expand this paper beyond addressing the headings.

4. Write the policy memo to all employees (for David Jones' signature) announcing the new extended hours policy and describing the shift structure that will support it.

5. Write a memo to all Widgets Я Us employees from President Evans describing and implementing your company's new ethics policy.

CHAPTER 7

Managing the Organization's Information Needs

A. Information and technology

B. Improving employee writing

C. Documenting processes and decisions

D. Documenting problems, solutions, and recommendations

E. Measuring and documenting progress and success

A. Information and Technology

> **One who knows the enemy and knows himself will not be endangered in a hundred engagements. One who does not know the enemy but knows himself will sometimes be victorious, sometimes meet with defeat. One who knows neither the enemy nor himself will invariably be defeated in every engagement.**
>
> —Sun-tzu, *The Art of War* (6th century BC, trans. Ralph Sawyer, New York: Barnes and Noble, 1994, 135)

No organization can exist efficiently without adequate information flow. In *The Art of War*, General Sun-tzu emphasized 2,600 years ago that information is critical to good decision making. However, equally important is the *quality* of the decision made on the foundation of knowledge.

Modern managers are bombarded by information—some critical to mission accomplishment, most of it simply confusing "noise" that distracts. Managerial writing must be carefully selective regarding the information chosen, processed, verified, and determined complete before actually using it in some form of communication with others. If the project or task is particularly complicated, the managerial writer might want to create an *information plan* to assist in this process.

Suppose you are interested in genealogy to the extent that you want to compile a small book on the history of the Johnson family. This is a *huge* undertaking and gives you many concerns. In addition to the mechanical process of writing a book, proofreading it, sending it to a publisher, and overseeing its distribution and sales (all *project* milestones), there is the sober-ing burden of finding *all* the ancestors back to a certain period, determining the accuracy and completeness of the information gathered, and getting help in the project. Also, you think this would be a good idea, but will enough family members buy the book to make it at least a break-even proposition? So you develop an information plan to determine whether you can actually get, process, and verify the accuracy and completeness of the information you will need to make the project a reality.

I. Purpose for Writing: To provide a written history and genealogy of the Johnson family from 1730 to the present for sale and distribution to family and historical organizations.

II. Audience: Current members of the Johnson family, local historical society

III. Goals of Information: Information gathered for this writing project will support the development of an accurate and complete record of the Johnson family since they moved to Gulf, North Carolina, in 1730.

IV. Information Objectives:

- Obtain accurate birth, marriage, children, and death records for each generation.

- Locate and develop anecdotal information about each lineal ancestor and that ancestor's immediate family.

- Research pertinent facts concerning historical events occurring during each generation and how those facts (the War Between the States, for example) affected that generation.

- Obtain photographs, portraits, drawings, and sketches of family members, their homes, and other items (such as furniture) related to each generation.

V. Methodology: Information collection tasks will be divided according to the four objectives. Four family members have each agreed to be the primary focus for one task and will coordinate their efforts with the other three. They will form a commit-tee, and interested members of the family throughout the United States will provide all relevant information to the specific committee member responsible for that kind of information. When enough information is gathered to produce a draft, Jeannie Johnson will write it, coordinate it with the other members of the committee, and then send it to those members of the family who contributed information. After this family review, the final corrections and additions will be made and the book will be published. The committee will offer subscriptions to underwrite publication cost; from

continued

this information, the committee will produce 10 percent more books than ordered to accommodate those who change their minds later.

VI. Information Specifications:

- Birth, death, marriage, and issue information must be from official sources or verified by at least one other source to be considered "firm" rather than "tentative."

- Generation stories must be documented by notation as to *who* said *what* about an ancestor, *when* it was said, and *how* it was known. "Traditional" stories may be used if labeled as such, but every effort must be made to identify the *source* and *accuracy* of the story.

- Only events and activities actually affecting a particular generation should be developed for the book. For example, the flu epidemic of 1917 affected most Americans—did any Johnson contract or die from the flu?

- Identification of subjects of photographs, portraits, and related graphic items must be documented. The time period and circumstances surrounding the picture should be described wherever possible.

VII. Content Outline:

- Jeannie Johnson will prepare a mockup of the proposed book layout (using a four-part approach of individual information, photo/portrait, anecdotes, and historical background) after sufficient information has been obtained to trace some activity of the family in each generation back to 1730.

- Each committee member is responsible for ensuring that all information under his or her responsibility is reported accurately, is as complete as possible, and is put in its proper place in the mockup.

VIII. Information Verification:

- Each bit of information received will be validated through (1) requiring the submitter to include the source and (2) cross-checking other sources where possible.

- All members of the Johnson family subscribing to this project are equally responsible for information verification through editorial and content review of the resulting draft.

IX. Schedule of Milestones:

- Jan 20xx: Obtain prepublication subscriptions
- Jan 20xx: Assemble all known data; identify areas requiring research

continued

- Jan 20xx: Begin birth/death/marriage event review (courthouse, family records)
- Jan 20xx: Begin anecdote search (family records)
- Jan 20xx: Begin photo/portrait search (family records)
- Jan 20xx: Begin world/local history search (history books, family records)
- Mar 20xx: Verify birth/death/marriage event data
- Mar 20xx: Verify anecdote data
- Mar 20xx: Verify photo/portrait data
- Mar 20xx: Verify world/local history data
- Mar 20xx: Complete records review
- Apr 20xx: [incorporate all corrections; publish] <u>NO! Not an info milestone</u>

X. Assumptions and Dependencies:

- Assumption: Publicity will create enough interest in this project to fund the publication.
- Dependency: Production of a book containing this information requires funding through Johnson family member prepublication subscription.

Note the tendency to add *project* milestones to the *information* ones—they belong in a project plan, of which the information plan would be a part.

To make a point about the surfeit of information managers are faced with, consider this puzzle:

1. There are five houses; the physicist lives next to the man with the horse.
2. The Spaniard owns a dog; there are coffee drinkers in the green house.
3. The Belgian drinks tea; the chemist lives next to the man with the fox.
4. The green house is immediately to the right of the white house.
5. The mathematician owns a cat; there are milk drinkers in the middle house.
6. The German lives in the red house; a physicist lives in the yellow house.
7. The biologist drinks orange juice; the Norwegian lives in the first house.
8. The Japanese is an engineer; the Norwegian lives next to the blue house.
9. Each man has one house, a different nationality, a different pet, a different occupation and a different choice of drinks.

Who Owns the Zebra? Who Drinks Water?

This parlor game demonstrates a number of concepts useful when working with the information sets writers of managerial communication often are faced with: (1) quite often we *have* the whole picture, but it has been presented in bits and pieces that are difficult to piece together; (2) just as often, there are bits of information that we do not need and which might even sidetrack our progress toward creating order out of chaos. However, it is always difficult to determine what to do, especially with a time constraint.

Solving the zebra/water problem requires framing the information we have. Close examination determines that there are five houses of five different colors with inhabitants of five nationalities who have pets, beverages, and occupations. Consequently, you can *draw* this situation as a five-by-five-cell table, the five columns being numbered 1 through 5 and the five rows being labeled house color, nationality, occupation, pet, and beverage.

Now revisit the bits of information. There are milk drinkers in the middle house (fact number 5 and the Norwegian lives in the first house (fact 7). You may have some false starts along the way, but if you go from *fact* first to probability, you will fill in every cell and be absolutely certain of your answer.

Try the exercise and you will discover another unusual but profoundly important fact: you know who drinks water *and* who owns the zebra *before* you have filled in all the blank cells. That is significant because almost everyone who works this out completes filling in *all* of the cells before stopping. That was *not* the task. Quite often we stop to fill in too many blanks and thus delay a recommendation that could be late in a time-constrained situation. The results of stopping to smell the roses in a business setting can be deadly. Do not be sidetracked by the temptations of too much information.

Technology is an accelerant to the obtaining and processing of adequate information. However, it also is an accelerant to the *volume* of information you can access. A half-century ago, if you wished to research a problem, you went to a library and spent hours finding a handful of usable references to consult. Now you go onto the Internet with a search engine and in seconds find over a million "hits." To be sure, they are automatically sorted in order of relevance; however, even with the volume of data on your screen, you are still faced with the issues of accuracy, relevance, and completeness.

Software programs enhance our ability to sort, process, and display information. A spread sheet will produce charts and graphs on simple commands, and a text file will display word count, occurrence of specific words, and even grammar and spelling errors instantly. Publishing programs will produce illustrated newsletters and fact sheets that permit the creator to move objects such as text boxes and graphics at will and reshape them in the process. However, technology applications are like walking versus driving a race car: if you are not skilled as a driver, the speed can cause you more problems than you bargain for. In short, a half-century ago, external managerial communications were written, reviewed by management layers, and then traveled by courier or by mail; today, they require pressing the Enter key and are not subjected to an external review process. It is quite possible today for a worker to *be* the company—before the senior managers ever realize what just happened via a message the worker sent.

B. Improving Employee Writing

The manager has a singular reason for actively engaging in improving his or her employees' writing: the efficiency and productivity of the organization depend upon the accuracy, speed, and completeness of the information flow.

For employees to be effective in their writing, they must be able to analyze and to write. Merely having the ability to write messages in "proper" English is not enough. The communication *must* inform and persuade the reader *appropriately* without causing an unanticipated and detrimental reaction.

The axiom holds true even in this century: to write well, a writer must *read* and *write* copiously and at all opportunities. Managers should give their workers every opportunity to write and also to read what others have written. To assure uniformity in workplace writing, many managers either adopt or develop a style manual relevant to their organization. If the style manual has to be created, a wise manager engages his or her employees in the process of creating it. As a result, the employees "own" the manual and will become stronger writers because they know firsthand what is expected of them.

C. Documenting Processes and Decisions

A manager in a busy organization would do well to commission his or her employees to create a procedure manual that covers the duties associated with every position within the organization. With such a manual in place, if a key worker suddenly becomes ill or leaves the organization, another can step in with little or no training and take over the duties effectively. This is a fundamental type of documentation that the manager should ensure is in place. The typical documentation for a *process* is separated into headings for each step of the process with a narrative or series of steps to describe what must be done at each stage/step of the process.

A *flow chart* can also describe a process in an office that involves decision points and alternative routes. Here is a simple chart to illustrate a a flow chart. This particular flow chart was created with a tool sold by Edraw Soft (http://www.edrawsoft.com/Process-Flowcharts.php):

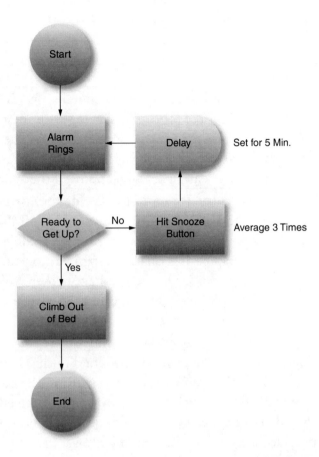

Start

Alarm Rings → Delay Set for 5 Min.

Ready to Get Up? No → Hit Snooze Button Average 3 Times

Yes

Climb Out of Bed

End

Human Resource managers learned early that personnel rules and regulations are complex and unforgiving; consequently, they created a series of "decision logic tables" that list specific situations their clients might find themselves in and the various alternatives, given that situation. As a consequence, key decisions will be made the same way whenever the circumstances call for department action of a specific nature. Here is a sample from the U.S. government's Office of Personnel Management:

Instructions for Processing Personnel Actions

The chapters in the **Guide** will tell you how to select the codes and information to enter on the Standard Form 52, Request for Personnel Action. If you do not have all the information you need about the reason for the action or about the employee it concerns, **ASK QUESTIONS** of the personnel specialist who approved the action. **DO NOT GUESS.** Your documentation affects the rights and benefits of Federal employees.

continued

Follow the 3 steps in the table below when processing personnel actions.

STEP	ACTION
1	Decide what kind of action has been requested or is needed. Most personnel actions are processed starting with the receipt of a Standard Form 52, Request for Personnel Action. Check blocks 5-B and 6-B in Part B. If you cannot tell from the Standard Form 52, ask the personnel specialist who approved the action.
2	Locate the correct chapter in the **Guide** for instructions on processing the action. Use the reader aids, the Table of Contents and the Topic Index (Chapter 34), in the **Guide** to choose the most likely chapter. If terms are unfamiliar to you, refer to the Glossary (Chapter 35). Once you have chosen a likely chapter, review the chapter contents page and the coverage section for that chapter. These will help you decide whether the instructions you need are contained in the chapter.
3	Follow carefully the instructions found in the chapter(s) appropriate for the action you wish to process. Read the narrative information included in the chapter before going to the tables and figures. Provided in each chapter are definitions for terms used. Also provided are instructions that refer to special situations that may occur which the tables and figures may not address.

Source: http://www.opm.gov/feddata/gppa/gppa02.pdf.

For more complex decision choices, tables with multiple columns can be developed and, of course, this methodology is not limited to personnel decisions.

D. Documenting Problems, Solutions, and Recommendations

Managers employ a number of ways to document problems, solution, and recommendations. One of the most common ways is the Memorandum of Understanding (the MOU). There is no set format for such a document, although various organizations have developed their own versions (usually reviewed and approved by their General Counsel's office). The MOU should contain a *date* of creation and of activation, a *title* indicating its content, and a *signature* section listing the key parties to the agreement and their titles. Generally speaking, MOUs have a number of sections stating the *authority* under which the MOU is enacted, the *problem* or *area of agreement* involved, the *background*, and the *actions* or *obligations/responsibilities* of the parties.

A standard way to describe a problem and possible solution to a senior manager is via a point paper, fact sheet, issue paper, position paper, or white paper. Although these formats may vary slightly according to specific organization adaptation, they generally occur on one or two pages and indicate, in this order, an *issue*, *background* (or *discussion*), *possible courses of action*, and *recommended course of action*. An additional section on *impact* (of solution or of continuing with no solution) might also be included. These documents list the originator or point of contact with contact information and can result in, or be delivered at, a briefing on the issue. Any detailed documentation will be on an attachment, not part of the one or two-page summary.

Here is a sample Point Paper from Department of the Army OM-25-1-50, page 14:

OFFICE SYMBOL

DATE

Memorandum for XXX

From: (Name and Position Title) (Signature and Date)

Subject: Format Instructions—For Decision

1. PROBLEM. To revise decision staff paper format for the publication of OM 25-1-5, dated 1 Jun 01.

2. BACKGROUND AND DISCUSSION.

    a. Address all decision staff papers to CECS. Sign and date after coordination is completed.

    b. Paragraph 1. PROBLEM—Give reason for preparing decision paper. Be brief and direct. Indicate in parenthesis and in capital letters whether "decision" is time sensitive.

    c. Paragraph 2. BACKGROUND and DISCUSSION—Use this paragraph to further discuss above recommendations if their complexity requires it. Introduce here any document(s) used to support the recommended action(), summarizing key points, and attach as tab(s).

    d. Paragraph 3. IMPACT. Discuss here the resource impact of recommended decision.

    e. Paragraph 4. COORDINATION—Indicate coordination, CONCUR, or NONCONCUR. Enter coordinating officer(s) by name as shown in paragraph 4 below. If coordinating (CONCURRENCE/ NONCONCURRENCE) statements accompany the decision staff paper, identify them as tabs in the next paragraph.

    f. Paragraph 5. COORDINATING STATEMENT—Use this paragraph, as necessary, to correlate coordinating statements with tabs, as shown in paragraph 5 below.

    g. Paragraph 6. RECOMMENDATION—Use this paragraph to recommend specific action(s). For each recommended action, enter an approval line where approving authority may validate action.

NOTE: CECS stands for Civil Engineers Chief of Staff, OM is Operations Manual.

E. Measuring and Documenting Progress and Success

Progress reports can take many forms, but all have in common that they contain the TO, FROM, SUBJECT, and DATE information up front. The simplest form is a note to a supervisor, the next most common form is the Weekly (or other period) Activity Report (WAR). The WAR summarizes the successes and challenges of an individual organization during the period covered. A higher office consolidates these reports and passes a summary to the CEO or other senior authority so that person (or steering group) has a snapshot of the highlights within the entire organization for the period covered. Such reports tend to "accentuate the positive," as an old Fred Astaire song once advised, so although they are generally classified as *information* reports, they should be considered *persuasive* and positive in nature.

A more complicated project may require the manager to produce incremental Progress Reports that law out the goal of the project, the steps requires to complete the project, and the status of activity on each of the required intermediate steps or actions. Often this type of report (which contains sections with headers) includes a Gantt Chart or a PERT (Program Evaluation Review Technique) diagram (both explained in this section) to lay out the progress and remaining effort graphically.

A *Gantt chart* is a type of bar chart that illustrates a project schedule. Gantt charts illustrate the start and finish dates of the terminal elements and summary elements of a project and the dependency relationships between activities. Gantt charts can be used to show current schedule status using percent-complete shadings and a vertical "TODAY" line.

If you do not possess expensive Gantt-producing software, there are two easy ways to create a Gantt chart to incorporate in the status report for a project in this class: (1) use free software, or (2) create a table in MS Word or Corel WordPerfect. One free Gantt chart creator is found on http://www.ganttproject.biz and an example of its output appears below:

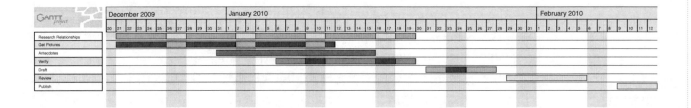

This is the Johnson Genealogy Project, for which we created an Information Plan earlier. Note that the entire project is addressed in this depiction, not merely the collection, processing, and verification of the information involved. Note also that the actual Gantt chart for a complex project would have many more elements and the resulting interdependences would also be included. This depiction of a project leads to a *network diagram*, also called a *PERT chart* (Program Evaluation Review Technique) or *critical path method* (CPM) chart. All of these techniques are used in project management, together with Lean Manufacturing concepts, including Six Sigma. If you are writing for managers using any of these applications, you should become thoroughly familiar with them.

To insert a Gantt chart from this program into your text file, export it as a JPG file and paste it in as a picture.

You can create a simple Gantt chart by creating a table in MS Word or Corel WordPerfect. Because this involves creating a cell for each unit of time, we will reduce the detail to weeks and create a 13 × 9 cell table (which is *not* as precise as the Gantt Project software, but will do for our report).

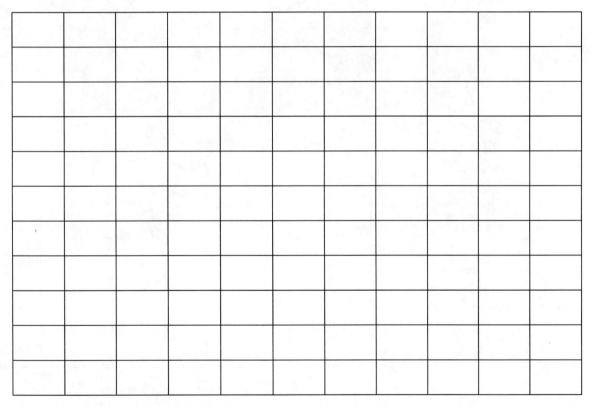

Now we adjust the cell width and fill in the X and Y axes with information:

JOHNSON FAMILY BOOK										
Week	1	2	3	4	1	2	3	4	1	2
Research Family										
Get Pictures										
Anecdotes										
Verify										
Draft										
Review										
Publish										

Finally, we can adjust lines, color cells to represent durations, and remove the lines between the cells that are colored to represent the activities (using the "merge cells" command). Here is the finished product:

JOHNSON FAMILY BOOK	Dec				Jan				Feb	
Week	1	2	3	4	1	2	3	4	1	2
Research Family										
Get Pictures										
Anecdotes										
Verify										
Draft										
Review										
Publish										

Note that the activities that take less time than the time period selected (in this example, one week) lose their accuracy in this scale; however, using a cell to represent a day would create a 76-cell width, which, if reduced to fit on a page, would result in a Gantt chart that would be too small to read.

Summary

In this chapter, we have considered ways to manage the organization's information needs. We have examined the impact of the information explosion and technology that can tame or encourage its proliferation. The manager has an urgent need to improve employee writing, because that improves the accuracy, completeness, and timeliness of information flow within and from/to the organization.

Documenting processes and decisions becomes easier when these activities are reduced to simple procedures using information organization tools such as tables and guidelines. The documenting of processes and decisions also yields to the application of standard formats, as does the measurement and documenting of organizational progress and success.

POTENTIAL ASSIGNMENTS

1. Select a complex project (your final paper in class or some assignment at work, for example) and create an information plan with the ten sections presented in this chapter. Be careful to list only *information* milestones (with dates) in that section, and remember that your plan for verification must be specific—no verifying the data by "verifying" it, please.

2. Create a point paper on some *real* issue (perhaps a problem you will propose a solution to in a more extensive researched proposal to submit to a decision maker in your organization or community).

3. Develop the first four or five pages of a style annual for your organization or for some organization you volunteer with (the Garden Club, PTA, etc.) providing writing guidelines for members to employ and samples of correspondence formats.

4. Produce a Weekly Activity Report to submit to your teacher outlining the successes and challenges you have experienced during the past week.

5. Assume that as a final paper for this course, you are presenting a researched proposal to a decision maker in your organization or community regarding some major issue or problem facing the organization. Develop a detailed progress report for the decision maker, describing (with headings) the progress made, challenges to yet overcome, and the remaining steps before the proposal is completely developed and submitted.

6. Create a Gantt chart describing the activities involved in producing the researched proposal described in Assignment 5.

CHAPTER 8

Developing Writing Skills Throughout Your Career

A. Writing opportunities

B. Job descriptions and career objectives

C. Developing a management philosophy

D. Collaborative writing

E. Social media opportunities

> **If you want to restore a Druid priesthood, you cannot do it by offering prizes for Druid-of-the Year. If you want Druids, you must grow forests.**
>
> —Arrowsmith, W. (1967)

Introduction

The opportunity to become a genuinely *good* writer is not the result of a single door opening to a single new horizon. Developing good writing requires considerable, consistent, and continuing effort. One of the most obvious things a writer must do is *read*. Reading brings to your eyes the principles that make good writing so, and with constant reading, you will absorb more than a text book can bring to you.

Along the way, you will find others who will benefit from your experience. Stop to teach them as you go.

Clear writing begins with clear thinking. It is possible to think clearly and still be thrown off track by buzzwords, jargon, colloquialisms, and other traps, but is simply impossible to correct those errors if the thinking that drove the writing was not clear in the first place.

This is true for you as you work to improve your own writing, and it is also true for others whose writings affect your work life. Have you noticed that those who think clearly around you are also the ones who can write clearly—and often the ones who gain more responsibility and earlier promotions?

The Druid-producing forests in your life are the opportunities you find to develop your writing skills. As long as you hover near fill-in-the-blank form reports and pro forma messages, you will not grow. Seek an environment where there is a need for good writing, and that environment will nurture you.

A. Writing Opportunities

Blot out, correct, insert, refine
Enlarge, diminish, interline.
Be mindful, when invention fails
To scratch your head and bite your nails.

—Jonathan Swift (1667–1745), *On Poetry*

Good writing—writing that is clear, concise, and to the point—does not happen accidentally. Like the musician's response to the tourist in New York City, who asked how could he get to Carnegie Hall, the answer is "practice, son, practice." Therefore, seek out opportunities to write and opportunities to be mentored by people you respect for their writing abilities.

Remember that what you write the first time may not be succinct enough or to the point. Blaise Pascal once apologized in a letter, "I have only made this letter longer because I have not had the time to make it shorter" (*Lettres Provincials*, http://dangerousintersection.org/2006/04/12/more-time-shorter-letter/).

B. Job Descriptions and Career Objectives

Career planning is the responsibility of every employee, but also rests squarely on the shoulders of the manager in regard to the people he or she supervises. Truly, planning ahead is a hallmark of the manager, so the manager's writing skills must include the ability to help his or her employees plan for the future.

In the workplace, a job description can be a useful tool in helping the manager know what to expect from an employee and how to help the employee remain focused on the deliverables in the specific job he or she has been assigned.

An effective and responsible manager helps each employee set and work for personal professional career goals. The goals should be written and the subject of periodic discussion so they can be adjusted, if necessary, and measurements taken of how they are progressing toward accomplishment. One effective management strategy is to employ Management by Objectives to build a framework of reliance on planning.

C. Developing a Management Philosophy

Remember what we proposed in Chapter 1: the purpose of *all* business writing is to persuade, and the purpose of managerial writing, in particular, is to change lives. Such writing must be clear, to the point, and create *only* the desired effect. As a manager, you can create the atmosphere for your subordinates by practicing good writing habits yourself and by guiding your subordinates to do likewise. Set the standard, and they will follow. Cultivate a management philosophy that teaches others to write by example and then encourages every employee to write, write, write!

D. Collaborative Writing

Some managers believe that collaborative writing is the ultimate corporate writing strategy. It is indeed a powerful tool and one that a practical manager will use frequently. Assigning sections of a complex and time-sensitive writing project to individual members of a team is an efficient way to develop a report or proposal quickly and without the risk a single writer faces in not paying sufficient detail to some important aspect because of the burden of contemplating the whole.

However, collaborative writing can be mismanaged, and the result is organizational disaster. Consider what goes into making a cake: you mix the appropriate portions of flour, eggs, milk, sugar, flavoring, and yeast. Some managers figuratively serve the pan full of raw ingredients without baking it at the prescribed temperature for the specified time.

So it is with group writing. No matter how closely attuned the writers may be to one another, the resulting document has many voices and no coherent theme unless one writer is designated to pull the pieces together, stir, *and bake* to produce a chemical change that will satisfy the palate and the reader. Textbooks with multiple authors are excellent examples of this principle: such authors are like-minded, effective writers with a single mission. However, it is the textbook editor's place to make them sing in perfect harmony—presenting you with a seamless testimonial regarding what works and what does not in the complex arena of a specific discipline.

Unmanaged group writing does *not* work; to paraphrase "Sam, I am," it doesn't work on a plane, it doesn't work on a train. It doesn't work at a government agency, it doesn't work in the military services, at the Pentagon, or in private industry, *unless* the group input is subjected to single-focused editing by one with the authority to override the outcry of prideful authors. That is how your author handled a $1.6 billion joint service budget successfully for eight years, editing and changing input from each military service—it's amazing how the question, "Do you want *your* words, or do you want money?" makes grownups rethink wordsmithing.

One prominent company that used a group to produce proposals for government contracts never employed a senior editor to create a whole product. Senior management soon discovered that the company was losing every contract they had spent hours going after. The law firm that produces a group opinion will cause every partner to out "weasel-word" (qualify) his subordinate until the result says nothing, if someone in the firm is not designated the lead for that group project.

It's interesting, isn't it, that most managers would never dream of creating a widget without designating a team leader, but often do not consider the implications of leaderless writing.

Be mindful when you employ collaborative writing to put the icing on the cake—*after* the ingredients are well-stirred and baked.

E. Social Media Opportunities

The electronic age has flooded the world with texting, blogs, tweets, and all manner of shorthand communication systems. Precisely like the teletype of nearly two centuries ago, these new media require the writer to abbreviate to save time and money. It hasn't taken long (as usual) for the earlier generation (our current "senior citizens") to comment on the "modern" communication standard. Here is a sample of STC (Senior Texting Code).

ATD: At The Doctor's
BYOT: Bring Your Own Teeth
CBM: Covered By Medicare
CUATSC: See You At The Senior Center
FWIW: Forgot Where I Was
LMDO: Laughing My Dentures Out
ROFL … CGU: Rolling On the Floor Laughing … And Can't Get Up[1]

Just as the teletype and ham radio have evolved, so will cell phone chatter mature and abbreviations give way to "real English" once again. However, here is the real lesson from any type of truncated communication: communication in *any* language, including English, is achieved by transmitting clusters (phrases) arranged in some sort of expected order. So, if "LOL" means "lots of laughs," and everyone agrees, then the shorthand is effective. Doctors and nurses have communicated on patient charts this way for years, as have composers when communicating emphasis and feeling to a chorus reading sheet music, mathematicians, and scholars citing sources. Of course, in STC, "LOL" means "Living on Lipitor," and in telegraphese "LOL" meant "Lots of Luck."

---

1   Bill Miller, Sr., *Missourian Editor*, January 5, 2011 (http://www.emissourian.com/opinion/columns/article_32f6d1a2-18d6-11e0-8910-001cc4c03286.html).

Because we communicate in clusters, it is possible to speed-read and it is possible to create a set of text abbreviations to make communication more rapid and more exact. Because all language is dynamic, it is also possible to see the evolution of each "improvement," which actually amounts to an ongoing adjustment of language to meet a new generation's requirements. Hence, "silly" in Shakespeare's day meant "wise," and "bad" to twenty-first-century teens means "awesome."

Words change meaning, conventions tweak usage, and when the dust of the eons settles, *clear, concise* communication still "rules." The clusters still work for a group in only one way (for example, misusing an idiomatic expression like "full of fluff" to become "full of flour" as one manager did, causes nothing but confusion) and all the clusters *must* be used in ways expected by the reader, or the communication will be in peril.

Summary

To become a *good* writer, and then to become a *better* writer, a manager must seek writing opportunities, read copiously, and consider always how to make his or her writing more clear, concise, and careful. Career planning is the responsibility of every manager. In the workplace, a job description can be a useful tool in helping the manager know what to expect from an employee and how to help the employee remain focused on what the deliverables are in the specific job he or she has been assigned.

Managers should work to develop a management philosophy that incorporates valuing writing in themselves and in those they supervise. Collaborative writing can be a useful managerial tool, but *only* if the manager appoints a senior editor to make the group product "speak" with one voice and one focus. Social media opportunities for clear and effective writing abound in this electronic age. The astute manager uses the "modern" tools to help in the communication process.

POTENTIAL ASSIGNMENTS

1. Rewrite the JADE PMO memorandum (Chapter 2, Section A) in your own words. Make certain the result will have *only* the desired effect.

2. Develop a career plan for yourself. Base this one- to two-page document on what you have accomplished to date in your working life and add to it the steps you must take to continue to develop in your chosen career field.

3. Create a writing guide to be used in your workplace as an aid to your co-workers. In the guide, touch on at least five common writing mistakes that you have observed in your organization with an explanation as to what is not working correctly and a step-by-step "cure" for each problem.

4. With a teammate chosen from your group of students, write a four-topic instruction guide for workers that addresses office policy and sets out rules of behavior for the group.

APPENDIX A

Resources for Managerial Writing

1. The U.S. Air Force's *The Tongue and Quill*, or Air Force Handbook (AFH) 33-337. Download at http://www.e-publishing.af.mil/shared/media/epubs/AFH33-337.pdf. Each military service has a similar guide book that provides sample of writing formats and a discussion of concepts. They're a must for government writing and quite useful in private industry.

2. *U.S. Government Style Manual*, U.S. Government Printing Office, available as a download at http://www.gpoaccess.gov/stylemanual/browse.html. The contents (listed below) are focused on government writing; however, the rules are quite similar to private industry as a whole.

Document Title		File Format and Size	Print Copy Pages
Title Page Style Board Extract from Title 44, U.S.C. About This Manual GPO's Online Initiatives		Text 20 KB PDF 1.1 MB	I–XIII
Contents		Text 3 KB PDF 237 KB	XV
Chapter 1	Advice to Authors and Editors	Text 7 KB PDF 690 KB	1–5
Chapter 2	General Instructions	Text 37 KB PDF 1.3 MB	7–26
Chapter 3	Capitalization Rules	Text 36 KB PDF 547 KB	27–42
Chapter 4	Capitalization Examples	Text 85 KB PDF 665 KB	43–77
Chapter 5	Spelling	Text 9 KB PDF 569 KB	79–94
Chapter 6	Compounding Rules	Text 30 KB PDF 542 KB	95–107
Chapter 7	Compounding Examples	Text 5 KB PDF 1.1 MB	109–191

Chapter 8	Punctuation	Text 58 KB PDF 1.1 MB	193–219
Chapter 9	Abbreviations and Letter Symbols	Text 31 KB PDF 682 KB	221–258
Chapter 10	Signs and Symbols	Text 10 KB PDF 1.1 MB	259–264
Chapter 11	Italic	Text 8 KB PDF 692 KB	265–268
Chapter 12	Numerals	Text 24 KB PDF 732 KB	269–280
Chapter 13	Tabular Work	Text 26 KB PDF 591 KB	281–298
Chapter 14	Leaderwork	Text 5 KB PDF 498 KB	299–302
Chapter 15	Footnotes, Indexes, Contents, and Outlines	Text 11 KB PDF 704 KB	303–308
Chapter 16	Datelines, Addresses, and Signatures	Text 23 KB PDF 786 KB	309–319
Chapter 17	Useful Tables	Text 1 KB PDF 828 KB	321–341
Chapter 18	Geologic Terms and Geographic Divisions	Text 3 KB PDF 381 KB	343–370
Chapter 19	Congressional Record, Congressional Record Index	Text 141 KB PDF 1.3 MB	371–416
Chapter 20	Reports and Hearings	Text 11 KB PDF 1.8 MB	417–432
Index		Text 1 KB PDF 791 KB	433–453

3. U.S. Small Business Association, *Writing a Business Plan*, available at http://www.sba.gov/category/navigation-structure/starting-managing-business/starting-business/. The site also provides guidance on writing effective job descriptions, creating employee handbooks, and emergency planning.

4. Purdue University also has a detailed explanation of how to write effective position descriptions, available at http://www.extension.purdue.edu/extmedia/EC/EC-728.pdf.

APPENDIX B

Samples of Managerial Communication

TASKING MEMO

DATE: 10/12/xx

TO: Tom Hastings

FROM: Jack Gilliam *J G*

SUBJ: Status of Mohair Project

Tom:

I need an in-depth review of the Mohair Project by COB[1] on the 22nd. Include a graphic showing cost to date and a time line for completion. Your report will be the basis for my defending the remaining budget.

---

1   COB stands for close of business.

MEMORANDUM FOR RECORD

September 29 2008

SUBJECT: Writing a Memo for Record

1.   The separate-page memorandum for record (commonly referred to as Memo for Record, MR, or MFR) is used as an informal, in-house document. It records information that is usually not recorded in writing (i.e., phone calls or meeting summaries) and passes it on to others. People working together generally pass information back and forth verbally, but sometimes it needs to be recorded and filed. A Memo for Record is perfect for this purpose. In addition, the informal format required by the MFR makes it the appropriate method for documenting day to day work center actions.

2.   The explanatory memo for record is another type of separate-page memorandum for record that is intended to accompany and explain the background of another, main memo. It tells who got involved and provides

continued

additional information not included in the basic memo. By reading both the basic memo and the explanatory memo for record, readers should understand enough about the subject to coordinate or sign the basic memo without having to call or ask for more information. If the basic memo really does say it all, an explanatory memo for record may not be needed.

3.   Type or write the Memo for Record on plain bond paper or squadron letterhead in this format. Use 1-inch margins all around and number the paragraphs if there are more than one. A full signature block is not necessary, but the MFR should be signed.

John N. Hancock, SSgt, USAF
1922CS/SC Shift Supervisor
(From http://www.airforcewriter.com/mfr.htm.
Copyright by Air Force Writer. Reprinted by permission.)

MEMORANDUM OF UNDERSTANDING

This document constitutes a Memorandum of Understanding (MOU) between _____ (your agency's name here) and local partners regarding _____ (name of project here). Those local partners are: _____ (list all local partners if one MOU or each separately if separate MOUs).

History

_____ (Your agency's name here) has worked with each of these local partners addressing _____ (an example is domestic violence). For the purpose of _____ (name of project here), each of these groups indicated a willingness to work with _____ (your agency's name here) to address the unique and varied concerns of this project.

Agency Roles and Responsibilities

Your Agency's Name

Describe your role and responsibilities for this project.

Local Partners

All local partners agree to provide those services detailed within this MOU. All local partners agree to coordinate the project activities of all local groups participating in

continued

their local portion of this project. All local partners agree to abide by federal and state guidelines regarding equal opportunity, drug-free workplace, and financial reporting.

Participating agencies' names, roles, and responsibilities as they relate to this project.

Planning and Development Team

The planning and development team will oversee all phases of this project's operation. Members of the team will include:

List all team members

This planning and development team will meet at least two times a year to coordinate each local partner's efforts.

Resources

Your agency's name here

List all resources that you will be contributing towards this project. For example: staff time, meeting space, supplies, etc.

List local partners here, along with all resources that they will be contributing towards this project.

I hereby agree to serve as the lead agency for my sections of this project, and I agree to abide by the terms and conditions contained in this Memorandum of Understanding between _____ (your agency's name here) and my agency for the purpose of _____ (project's name here).

_____

Name of individual, title, your agency's name

_____

Name of individual, title, agency's name

From http:www.gcc.state.nc.us/pubs/mou.pdf by the North Carolina Department of Crime Control and Public Safety.

INDEX